WORK FROM HOME ZONE

WORK
FROM HOME
ZONE

Helping entrepreneurs and employees
integrate work and life

Angela Crocker

Self-Counsel Press
(a division of)
International Self-Counsel Press Ltd.
Canada   USA

Self-Counsel Press acknowledges the financial support of the Government of Canada through the Canada Book Fund (CBF) for our publishing activities.

We also gratefully recognize the Coast Salish, Tsleil-Waututh, Squamish, Sto:lo, Musqueam, and Nooksack peoples, on whose land our offices are located.

Printed in Canada.

First edition: 2021

Library and Archives Canada Cataloguing in Publication

Title: Work from home zone : helping entrepreneurs and employees integrate work and life / Angela Crocker.

Names: Crocker, Angela, author.

Series: Self-Counsel business series.

Description: First edition. | Series statement: Business series

Identifiers: Canadiana (print) 20210299207 | Canadiana (ebook) 20210299231 | ISBN 9781770403376 (softcover) | ISBN 9781770405240 (EPUB) | ISBN 9781770405257 (Kindle)

Subjects: LCSH: Telecommuting. | LCSH: Telecommuting—Handbooks, manuals, etc. | LCSH: Flexible work arrangements. | LCGFT: Handbooks and manuals.

Classification: LCC HD2336.3 .C76 2021 | DDC 331.25/68—dc23

Every effort has been made to obtain permission and/or include the proper citations for quoted or referenced material or illustrations. If there is an omission or error, the author and publisher would be grateful to be so informed.

Self-Counsel Press
(a division of)
International Self-Counsel Press Ltd.

Bellingham, WA	North Vancouver, BC
USA	Canada

Contents

Notice to Readers

Laws are constantly changing. Every effort is made to keep this publication as current as possible. However, the author, the publisher, and the vendor of this book make no representations or warranties regarding the outcome or the use to which the information in this book is put and are not assuming any liability for any claims, losses, or damages arising out of the use of this book. The reader should not rely on the author or the publisher of this book for any professional advice. Please be sure that you have the most recent edition.

Dedication

For my home office co-workers, Paul and Sean, with love.

Acknowledgments

With an open heart and in the spirit of reconciliation, I acknowledge that I live, work, play, and learn on the traditional, ancestral, and unceded Indigenous land of the Coast Salish people including the kʷikʷəƛ̓əm (Kwikwetlem), xʷməθkʷəy̓əm (Musqueam), Sḵwx̱wú7mesh (Squamish) and səl̓ilwətaɬ (Tsleil-Waututh) Nations.

I am deeply grateful for the continued support of my family: those related — by blood, marriage, and choice. I send extra special appreciation to my husband, my son, my dad, and my brother, all of whom offer unconditional encouragement.

I'd also like to offer a shout out to my closest friends: Valerie, Kim, Peggy, Moira, Sue, Heather, Sam, Felice, Shelley, Vandhana, Vicki, Rebecca, Mike, Wilson, Elaine, Sharon, Janeen, Angela, Faye, Sylvia, and more. I've been blessed to know many of you for decades. Thank you for your ongoing support of me and my work.

I'd also like to thank my employers, clients, and students over the last 15 years. Our work together has given me a wealth of experience in working from home.

Introduction

At first glance, working from home shines as a romantic solution to many on-the-job problems. Ideally, you can eliminate your commute, reduce your childcare costs, avoid the seasonal germ fest, reduce annoying co-worker distractions, fit in more fitness, and, in some cases, be your own boss. While all these things are true to some extent, a sober second look sharpens the realities of how to integrate your professional life with your home life. It's not as easy as it seems but it is possible to thrive as you work from home. This book is filled with practical strategies and skills to help you do that.

The goal is to reduce friction between your work and the rest of your life. By finding ways to integrate the things you do every day with the work you need to accomplish, both areas of your life are enriched. In part, you'll look at how and when you spend your time. You'll also optimize the space you'll use for work and fine-tune the technology that enables you to do your job. Meanwhile, you'll find rhythm with the ebb and flow of daily life. This gives you the opportunity to prioritize the people and activities that are most important to you while still nurturing your professional life, or, at a minimum, earning an income to support your family.

1. Where We Work

Working from home is not a new concept. My grandfather, for example, ran a successful bookkeeping practice from his home starting in the 1960s until his death in the 1980s. During those same years, political volunteers, civil rights organizers, seamstresses, an army of Avon and Tupperware sales representatives, and many others worked from home.

As computer technology was developed, it became increasingly possible for families to have an in-home computer. While the computers of the early '80s were not nearly as capable as today's laptops, they did allow for word processing, spreadsheets, and other data entry. At the same time, the World Wide Web was maturing. Home access to the internet evolved from dial-up connections to high-speed. All of this technology made it feasible for even more of the workforce to work at home or, in many cases, for better or worse, to take work home.

In 2020, more workers than ever before experienced the work-from-home life for the first time as a result of the COVID-19 pandemic. The opportunity was thrust upon them as health officers ordered the immediate closure of workplaces in many public health regions. While this abrupt change was a stressful transition, workflows adapted to remote work and, in turn, remote workers adapted to working at home.

Many employers who, in the past, had resisted their employees working offsite learned that productivity remained high and there were cost savings in terms of commercial real estate, security services, cleaning expenses, and more. Several major corporations such as Microsoft, TELUS, and others announced that the majority of their workforce will no longer routinely work from corporate offices. More and more companies are following their lead as commercial real estate leases expire and workers seek greater flexibility. Some want to work from home full-time while others desire a hybrid model with some at-home days and some in-office days. Moving forward, working from home as a standard business practice is now an option for many categories of employees.

Admittedly, not all jobs can be done from home, at least not entirely. Grocery stores, restaurants, and more must serve their customers in-person. While numerous retail outlets offer online shopping, there is still a demand for brick-and-mortar stores, even if only for warehousing stock and curbside order pick-up. Similarly, industrial jobs in construction, manufacturing, and food processing all require their skilled workers on site. Further, personal care services such as hair styling, pedicures, and relaxation massages aren't easily done at home.

Notably, first responders from paramedics to police officers to firefighters must be on the job, in person. Their medical counterparts in hospitals, diagnostic services, medical clinics, and complementary medicine provide mainly face-to-face care for their patients, even when some telehealth appointments are possible.

However, even businesses that provide in-person goods and services likely have some staff that can work from home, at least some of the time. Consider the work of business administrators in finance, human resources, marketing, and so on. In some cases, part of that work can be done from home so employees have the option to split their time between a home office and a company's business address. How does a hybrid workweek sound to you?

Meanwhile, entrepreneurs have more control over how and where they work. Often they work from home during the start-up phase because the business cannot yet afford office space or commercial premises. But not all entrepreneurs move their work outside their home when resources allow. Many design their businesses assuming their global headquarters will remain in their homes to reduce commute time, increase available working hours, accommodate childcare and eldercare, or for health reasons. In some cases, the decision is made based on real estate prices. The cost of a home in a suburban neighborhood or a smaller town is much lower than urban centers or high-value real estate markets like New York and Vancouver.

2. Writing from Experience

I've been working from my home headquarters since 2009. At various times, I've worked for myself or for an employer from my home office. Sometimes, I've done both at the same time with a part-time job and part-time client work. My employment has included paid work and volunteer work in both the for-profit and not-for-profit sectors. From big organizations to small businesses, I've worked within several industries.

My clients included many small businesses and solo entrepreneurs so I've seen an unusual number of home office configurations. From gloriously messy artists' studios to clinical in-home physiotherapy setups to dining-room table takeovers, I've seen it all. Some of these spaces are filled with garage sale furnishings while others are the elegant, functional product of an interior designer's handiwork. Suffice it to say, no two home offices are alike!

The Canadian Internet Registration Authority (CIRA) conducted research into Canadians' internet use. The report, Canada's Internet Factbook 2020, affirms that I'm not the only Canadian who finds benefit in working from home. The report states, "Despite not necessarily choosing to do so, many of us are seeing the benefits of working remotely. More than three-quarters say that spending less time commuting is the top benefit, but two-thirds say they are saving time in general. Fifty-four per cent of Canadians feel they've achieved a better work-life balance and half are enjoying better flexibility with doing chores and errands." See www.cira.ca/resources/factbook/canadas-internet-factbook-2020.

In my own work-from-home experiences, I've navigated the challenges of sharing space with a spouse who is also working from home. I've done this through a series of parenting phases — from toddler to teenager — each with its own necessary accommodations. As a member of the sandwich generation, I navigated complex dementia care and hospice care for family elders. Ultimately, I acted as executor to settle two of their estates: an extra full-time job! During those same years, I faced some difficult medical issues that were, thankfully, resolved with surgery after five years of struggle. The only way my professional life survived was to integrate my work with the rest of my life.

Let me be transparent: I made mistakes along the way. I didn't start out with an idyllic revenue-generating work-from-home career and, in all honesty, not every year has been profitable. Some mistakes cost me time and money and non-work priorities meant I missed out on opportunities. Some of those were hard lessons to learn. I'll never forget the name of the client who refused to pay my final invoice when he found out I worked from home and, as a result, he felt I couldn't be in business "for real." Grr!

The good news is I've figured out a lot of what works for me through trial and error and I'll share those lessons in this book. I also found a community of professional colleagues navigating the same juggling act. Peers can be wonderfully supportive and a deep well of information to lift one another up. As the women's movement so elegantly declares, together we rise. Everyone's work-at-home journey is unique. Yours will be, too, and I hope I can lift you up as you find your way.

3. Consulting the Experts

To enrich the advice in this book, I've surveyed and interviewed others who also work from home and those whose professional expertise is particularly relevant. Some are remote workers for big corporations. Others are self-employed entrepreneurs building businesses around great ideas and inventions. A few are full-time employees who run a side hustle at home to earn extra income. Still more are building their professional lives through franchises or network marketing businesses. And then there are the volunteers who contribute their time and talents without drawing a salary. The one thing they all have in common? A home office.

Throughout the book, you'll find lived experiences from these work-from-home workers. In some cases, I'll quote their words directly and credit their comments using first and last names. Others wanted to share their stories on the condition of anonymity. Of course, I've honored their requests. In these situations, I'll share their ideas using a first name only; some will be real while others are pseudonyms. A desire for privacy doesn't diminish the value of their perspectives and examples.

Collectively, I'm grateful to have had access to so much earned and learned wisdom to add to my own thoughts.

4. Why Work from Home?

Just as there are many different types of work that can be done from home, there are at least that many reasons why you might decide to do it. Respondents to my work-at-home survey shared the catalyst that prompted them to work from home. Instantly, I saw several common themes. Let's take a closer look to see if any of them resonate for you.

4.1 Employment opportunities

We all work to earn a living. Whether we seek a job to pay the bills or a placement to advance our careers, finding meaningful work is a leading catalyst for accepting a work-at-home position. The opportunities for each employee or entrepreneur vary according to their circumstances:

- Executive human resources consultant Brian wasn't able to "find suitable employment as an employee" so he created his own business to earn an income.

- Similarly, recent business graduate Leslie "found it was easier to find a contract position [than] a J.O.B." Contract work from home, in this case.

- Information technology (IT) analyst Paul shared that his employer has all IT team members work from home most of the time. Their hybrid model creates flexibility for employees to spend a few days each month at clients' offices but only when necessary.

- Karine struggled to find a conventional full-time job when she moved from Toronto to Vancouver. She built a consulting business to take on contract work instead.

- Vancouver-based Sharon found her "desire to be an entrepreneur" after her banking job "was centralized to Toronto." Today, she runs a successful "company that manufactures baby soft goods" from her suburban home.

- Relocating to help family prompted Carla to move "from [San Francisco] to Orlando to help family" knowing that the job market in Orlando was limited. She tapped into her stronger "personal network in SF" to establish a career with more "flexibility to travel."

4.2 Family obligations

Many people work at home to accommodate family. Childcare costs, eldercare responsibilities, and supporting family members with disabilities are all catalysts that make working from home appealing. Done well, workers can earn a living and concurrently fulfill their family obligations.

- Eileen noted that she was expecting her first baby and her employer did not want "to give [her] a flexible schedule to accommodate a daycare situation."

- Katherine switched employers so that she could "be home with [her] children."

- Nicole, academic researcher and single mother of four, works from home to accommodate "parenting demands." This allows her to work full time while still providing meals, transportation, discipline, fun, and more for her kids.

- Childcare was expensive and largely unavailable in Ann's hometown. With four preschool and/or school-aged children, it "made more sense for [her] to work from home, given the age and number of children."

- Maria left her "teaching career to raise [her two] kids" and established a national women's business organization from her home office.

- When Rebecca became a single parent to her young child, working from home was the best available option.

- Jennifer discovered that "the cost of covering daycare [versus] income didn't make sense." She found that "super flexible" jobs with reasonable pay were "nonexistent" so starting her own home-based business was the obvious choice.

Parenting isn't the only family obligation you'll navigate. If you're part of the sandwich generation, you'll know that parenting responsibilities often overlap with caring for elderly parents. This leaves us scrambling to make sure everyone is safe, healthy, and happy — in that order of priority. It's a daunting task that takes a toll. (Be sure to read Chapter 15 for ways to bolster your social-emotional, mental, and physical health.)

I spent several years ensuring my grandmother was well looked after. As her medical needs progressed, she was unable to manage on her own but not yet ready for a care home. I took charge of her financial affairs, home maintenance, medical care, recreation activities, and social outings. A single 45-minute dentist's appointment would typically require 5 hours of my time. Thankfully, I could work (or rest) during the 45 minutes of the appointment.

Additionally, I managed communication between a team of doctors, care aides, paid companions, accessible transport drivers, public health nurses, family friends, and others — about 22 people in total. I was managing a team much larger than my company's staff roster without pay.

4.3 Medical reasons

For some workers, working from home makes sense to accommodate medical needs. Occasional sick days, ongoing chronic illness, or public health orders can move workers home temporarily or permanently. In some cases, such as cancer patients or those with autoimmune disorders, the risk of infection is too great. For others, it's about energy. Workers living with chronic fatigue, multiple sclerosis, or similar illnesses are less productive at the office when they use up their available energy commuting to work. Mobility can also be a factor. Patients with partial paralysis, amputations, and cumbersome mobility equipment may prefer to work from home where their specialized equipment is at hand.

- Claire, for example, started working at home due to her hip surgery. While her body was healing she couldn't drive and her walking mobility was limited. To accommodate her needs, her employer allowed her to work from home during her recovery.

- Michelle, a professional fundraising executive, thought she'd work in her downtown office throughout her pregnancy. However, complications at 30 weeks' gestation meant she had to rethink that plan. Rather than go on maternity leave ten weeks early, she made arrangements to work part time from home with her employer's support.

- Multiple sclerosis changed Cassidy's career profoundly. Her relapsing-remitting symptoms made it difficult to continue her career as an elementary school teacher. Undeterred, Cassidy earned her real estate license and established a thriving business from her home office in partnership with another REALTOR® who could look after clients when Cassidy's symptoms temporarily prevented her from working.

An unexpected regional (or global) health event may also require us to work at home. The COVID-19 pandemic, community measles outbreaks, or a spreading Zika virus are just three examples. While these events don't happen annually or even every decade, rapid spread of viral disease is always a possibility.

Under the Canadian Human Rights Act (CHRA), employers have a duty to accommodate workers with disabilities. The Canadian government defines disability as "a physical or mental condition that is permanent, ongoing, episodic or of some persistence, and is a substantial or significant limit on an individual's ability to carry out some of life's important functions or activities, such as employment. Disabilities include visible disabilities, such as the need for a wheelchair, and invisible disabilities, such as cognitive, behavioural or learning disabilities, and mental health issues." (See www.canada.ca/en/government/publicservice/wellness-inclusion-diversity-public-service/diversity-inclusion-public-service/working-government-canada-duty-accommodate-right-non-discrimination/duty-accommodate-general-process-managers.html) In turn, workers in the United States are protected by similar requirements to accommodate under the Americans with Disabilities Act (ADA). When it is healthy, safe, and a reasonable cost, one way disabilities can be accommodated is with an option to work from home. (See www.dol.gov/general/topic/disability/ada.)

4.5 Financial

Money can also be the catalyst for working from home. In some cases, it's about cost savings. Think about how much you pay for your commute whether that's a transit pass or fuel for your car, parking, and other vehicle expenses. Add to that the cost of business attire, meals out, replacing lost umbrellas, and so on.

In other cases, the financial catalyst is about the potential to earn a larger income with low overhead and related tax write-offs.

- For podcast producer Peggy, "cost savings [and] convenience" were central to her decision to work from home. Without commute expenses, she saves both time and money.

- In turn, professional writer Michael found that his "writing career started with remote freelance opportunities. It was both easier and more fulfilling looking for online gigs than it was to find a more traditional full-time writing/editing job locally."

- Similarly, Grace realized that "becoming an entrepreneur" would make financial sense for her business and her family.

- Web developer Sanjit found that "renting an office became too expensive" and moving his business to his home made his business more profitable.

- Similarly, Wendy initially moved her photography business to a live-work studio because "it was cheaper" but now she prefers having her office and studio at home.

- When Tandeep's employer "limited office space availability," he and his colleagues had to adapt to a hybrid work model; some days in the office and some days at home. In this case, the employer realized cost savings by reducing commercial space.

4.6 Job perks

Who doesn't love perks?! Job-related benefits can take many forms. Beyond the traditional extended health benefits and retirement savings, today's workers are discovering a wider range of perks that influence their decision to work from home.

- One of the attractive benefits of Kelsey's current job is the opportunity "for employees to take work-from-home days as needed." Imagine having the flexibility to meet the appliance repair tech, take an elder to a midday medical appointment, or be home for a delivery without having to use up a vacation day.

- Arts administrator Sue enjoys the hubbub of a local café as her "satellite office" where she works two or three days each week. In effect, this is an offsite work-from-home arrangement with a great-cup-of-coffee bonus.

- Meanwhile, Heather, a health services administrator, believes the clinic she works at will "allow more work-from-home options to support work-life flexibility" moving forward.

- IT Manager Kim works with "individuals ... located in different cities [and different time zones]." Rather than go to the office and sit "staring at [her] computer and tied to a headset all day long," her employer allows her to work from home to accommodate "more time zones, while not having the impact of having to leave the house."

- Mia runs a software company and they have "always been hybrid and it's a growing way to attract a larger pool of employees." So, in this case, human resources has identified an attractive job perk.

5. Bottom Line

The work-at-home lifestyle takes some getting used to. While giving up a long commute is a dream come true for many people, the realities of working from home can be overwhelming.

This book is for both entrepreneurs and employees. It's designed to get you thinking about the things that will impact your business and your life at home. Grouped by topic, it offers solutions to common problems and options to help you maximize the perks of working at home. You will need to experiment to figure out what works for you and your household. There's no one-size-fits-all solution.

Remember, not everyone is well suited to working from home. Author and consultant Vicki McLeod shared, "Some people thrive in a workplace structure and really prefer to keep home life separate. To be really successful working from home takes personal discipline, accountability, flexibility, and the ability to set boundaries and be self-directed. That doesn't suit everyone. For those that choose it though, or can adapt, it can be a really satisfying and fulfilling lifestyle."

My intention is that you'll find solutions that work for you in these pages. If you're just starting out, read the book from cover to cover. If you've already embarked on the work-from-home journey, dive into the chapters that will help you solve the problem you're facing today. You might take the advice as written or you might mix-and-match different ideas to create something that works for you.

Above all, these strategies aim to help you keep your equilibrium as your work-life shares space with the rest of your life. It's more about integration than balance or separation. After all, work is part of life, right?

Section 1
Finding Your Way

As you embark on your work-from-home journey, you enter into a professional world that's both familiar and different. If you make the choice, you'll have time to map out your next moves. If the choice is imposed on you by your employer or happens abruptly due to something such as a pandemic, you'll be scrambling, for a little while, at least.

Happily, the work-from-home life is filled with many new paths. You can still work for an employer or you can work for yourself. You can work entirely at home or set-up a hybrid arrangement with in-office days and at-home days. You'll also get to decide how much you work — part time? Full time? More than full time? It's up to you.

Figuring out the path that works for you gives you an opportunity to look at your life as a whole. You'll think about how work integrates with fitness and family, technology, and personal needs, and so much more. In many ways, you're living a "Choose Your Own Adventure" novel with lots of decisions to make the experience work for you.

1
What Does
"Work from Home" Mean?

Working from home is not one size fits all. For every job that can be done from home, there are a dozen or more ways to do that work. However, we can group those who work at home into three broad categories each with specific conditions related to the type of employment. These categories are remote work, entrepreneurial work, and hybrid work.

1. Remote Work

Remote workers are, typically, employees of a business. If you are an employee, you've been hired by a small business, a large corporation, or something in between. You are expected to do your job away from the company's business premises.

When doing remote work, you are one member of a larger team and your job responsibilities are itemized in your job description. The projects you manage and the related day-to-day tasks are all directed by the company. Of course, you have autonomy to complete your work as you see fit but you also have predetermined expectations, milestones, and deadlines to meet.

Most likely, you are required to provide your own workspace furniture: desk, chair, file storage, and so on. You may also be required to acquire your own technology while in other cases you'll be provided with the technology needed to do your job. Your gear requirements could include a laptop, mobile phone, webcam, and software subscriptions. If your employer provides technology or equipment, it remains the property of the company and must be surrendered to the employer when the staff member leaves that job.

Remote workers are often beholden to set office hours, in a particular time zone. So, if you live in Vancouver but work for a company headquartered in Toronto you might be expected to work from 6:00 a.m. to 2:00 p.m. (Pacific Standard Time) to correspond with Toronto-based colleagues working 9:00 a.m. to 5:00 p.m. (Eastern Standard Time). Other companies give employees more flexibility. TELUS employees, for example, can work their eight-hour day anytime between 7:00 a.m. and 7:00 p.m.; some start early and end early while others start late and end late. On really busy days, some workers will start early and end late making for a lengthy work day! Depending on family needs, some TELUS workers break up their day with blocks of time for work and family. You may love the opportunity to pick up your child from school every day, for example.

As Marketing Manager for Events Plus Management Ltd., Peggy Richardson promotes consumer shows including the two-day Westcoast Small Home Expo. She spends 90 percent of her time working remotely – at home and in her vehicle – and the balance of her time working onsite for events or in-office for scheduled meetings. Typically, she spends just four days each month in the office. Zipping around southern British Columbia in her vintage vehicle to visit clients and event locations, she's also accustomed to getting work done on the road – at rest stops, ferry terminals, and coffee shops. She quipped, "I specialize in McDonald's Wi-Fi." She has learned the optimal parking spaces to make the most of complimentary internet access, with hot cups of tea and, occasionally, hot fries delivered right to her vehicle. While Peggy makes herself available when clients need her on evenings and weekends, she mostly keeps conventional office hours to align with her partner's work schedule and their daughter's school day and competitive ballet schedule.

While working from home offers lots of flexibility, your days of work are still controlled by your employer. Your job contract, employment terms, and/or seniority will determine how many vacation days, sick days, personal days, and any other time off you are entitled to. Requests for leave must be approved by your supervisor and the human resources department.

Employees are paid on a set schedule. Depending on your employer's payroll policy, you'll receive a steady paycheck monthly, biweekly, or on some other interval. The payroll system will deduct taxes from your salary or hourly rate and take care of reporting that income to Canadian Revenue Agency (CRA), Internal Revenue Service (IRS), or a similar government body. You file taxes as an individual, not as a business.

2. Entrepreneurial Work

Entrepreneurial workers, typically, work for themselves. Their business efforts are self-directed. They may be self-employed as the owner of a business or, perhaps, someone who works as a representative for a network sales company such as Color Street, Rodan+Fields, or Discovery Toys.

When doing entrepreneurial work, you are in control of the projects, products, and services you work on. It's up to you to decide what ideas and opportunities you pursue and you take on all the associated risks: financial, reputation, liability, etc. You're also responsible for all the expenses of running the business from errors and omissions insurance to business license to human resource costs. If your work is successful you reap the rewards, and if it fails you absorb the losses. Day-to-day productivity to achieve success is up to you.

Elaine Tan Comeau is an entrepreneur based in Vancouver. For more than ten years, she has worked from home six days a week. She is the founder and CEO of Easy Daysies Ltd., as well as an author, speaker, and host of Elaine's Kitchen Table (the podcast named for the place where she started her business). Easy Daysies' success is indisputable with multiple award-winning products and it is one of the few companies ever to incite a bidding war amongst all five dragons on CBC's *Dragons' Den*. Elaine designed her business so that she can work from home at her kitchen table most of the time. This was a conscious choice so that she could work flexible hours which allow her to work around her children's schedules most of the time. She also has a desk at the company's warehouse facility where she can work, as needed. When necessary, she travels to meet with buyers across North America and for public appearances. Without question, Elaine and her company are a stellar example of the potential success possible when you work from home.

In addition to providing your own workspace, you have the added costs of running your business. Technology, furniture, and other home office supplies are all business expenses, a portion of which are tax deductible. You'll be responsible for payroll, if you have employees, and depending on location and income, will be required to collect taxes from your customers. (Consult the CRA, IRS, or applicable revenue agency in your area to inquire about businesses and taxation.)

Furthermore, product-based businesses will have inventory to manufacture, warehouse, and manage. Don't forget shipping supplies; all those boxes and packing tape add up! Meanwhile, service-based entrepreneurs will "stock" intellectual property such as lessons, speeches, ebooks, and more, plus their available time for billable one-on-one appointments, group meetings, and so on. Whether physical or intellectual, these items become assets of the business or, in other words, property of the entrepreneur.

As an entrepreneurial worker you set your own hours. Some industries require conventional 9:00 a.m. to 5:00 p.m. office hours while other industries allow the entrepreneur to work when it suits them. For example, a self-employed accountant might work 9:00 a.m. to 5:00 p.m., Monday to Friday, in alignment with banker's hours. In turn, a self-employed physiotherapist might work 3:00 p.m. to 7:00 p.m. from Wednesday to Sunday.

Many entrepreneurs end up working more than the traditional 40-hour week as they pursue their professional goals. This pace of work is not sustainable long term but it's common among entrepreneurs especially as they develop and launch new products and services. Other entrepreneurs set up shop with plans to work part time allowing them to juggle other responsibilities such as childcare, eldercare, and personal wellness.

Entrepreneurs are paid when the business is profitable. Once the company has a steady revenue stream, the entrepreneur draws a salary, be it monthly, biweekly, or on some other interval. However, the entrepreneur is responsible for remitting business taxes such as Canada's federal Goods and Services Tax (GST), Provincial Sales Tax (PST), or Harmonized Sales Tax (HST), or state taxes where applicable in the USA. In addition, the business must pay income taxes or corporate taxes to the Canadian Revenue Agency (CRA), Internal Revenue Service (IRS), or a similar government body.

Entrepreneurial business owners can structure their business in different ways, each with different financial risks, benefits, and obligations. In brief, a common business structure is a sole proprietorship, which is established when a person goes into business but there is no legal separation between their business finances and their personal finances. Alternatively, an incorporated business (inc.) or a limited liability partnership (LLP) creates a financial entity that's separate from the business owner's (or owners') personal finances. The latter protects the entrepreneur's personal assets.

3. Hybrid Work

Hybrid work offers the opportunity to work from home and work at the office. Both employees and entrepreneurs have the potential to work in a hybrid model. This means that they work some time each week in their home office and the balance of the week at their company's office or other commercial space. Let's look at some examples. These four women all do hybrid work from home offices in the Vancouver area:

- Shelley Neill is a full-time legal assistant with a personal injury law firm. She works from home one day a week, and this gives her the opportunity to focus on in-depth, detailed tasks without distraction. Meanwhile, four in-office days each week allow her to efficiently coordinate her caseload with colleagues.

- Sam Brulotte is an instructor with a college microbiology program. She works at the school three days a week setting up and teaching labs to nursing students. One day a week she does her marking from home. On the fifth day, she works from her car using a laptop and mobile phone data in the gaps between her children's activities: hockey, dance, and gymnastics.

- Vandhana Misri is a broadcast coordinator for a regional television station. She prefers to work in the office where she has several large computer monitors but works occasional days at home, when needed, to accommodate eldercare responsibilities. In addition, she runs a small business from her home on weekends, catering Kashmiri-style meals.

- Felice Bisby is the in-house graphic designer for a leading charitable organization. As part of her employment, she has the option to work from the office or from home. This hybrid approach helps her achieve a favorable work-life balance, accommodating family needs and work requirements throughout the week.

In many respects, hybrid workers have the best of both worlds; the conveniences and cost savings of their home office combined with the ease of communication and sense of community while working in a commercial space some of the time.

One of the key skills that hybrid workers must master is the art of transitioning work from one location to another. You'll need a workspace in both locations as well as your files and other information. Depending on the nature of your work, you might store your files in cloud storage or log into the company's server from wherever you are. For efficiency's sake, it's vital that you are working from the most recent version! All of this means that hybrid workers need to be highly organized and at least a little bit tech savvy to ensure they can do their work effectively in two or more locations.

4. Full Time or Part Time?

As you reflect on whether you will be a remote worker, entrepreneurial worker, or hybrid worker, think, also, about how much you want to work. What best suits your situation, full time or part time?

Take some time to reflect on your needs and wants. Do you need a job (or two) to pay the bills? Are you looking to advance your career? Are you living paycheck to paycheck? Do you aspire to earn more to save for your retirement, travel adventures, or some other dream? Most commonly, how much you work is determined by your financial obligations and your financial goals.

Your family situation can also influence your decision. Do you need to work around available childcare? Are you juggling eldercare responsibilities that limit your availability to work?

Your wellness needs may influence how much you work. How much work can your body handle? Does your mental health suffer if you work long hours?

Your decision may also be influenced by your stage of life. Are you a recent postsecondary graduate who aspires to full-time work to establish your career? Or are you a long-time worker approaching retirement who can get by with a part-time income at this stage in your life? Maybe you are a parent of a newborn or toddler without a daycare placement?

Keep in mind that it's not unusual for workers to have a full-time job plus a part-time gig or, at least, a side hustle. Similarly, you might hold down multiple part-time jobs to earn your living. Maybe you have a full-time, year-round job. In addition, you take on a seasonal position such as an accounting assistant job at tax time, or work as a retail store clerk helping holiday shoppers in December.

In his bestselling book *Side Hustle* (Currency, 2017), author Chris Guillebeau shares his 27-day plan to identify, develop, and launch a profitable idea. He defines a side hustle as "a money making project you start on the side, usually while still working a day job. In other words, it's a way to create additional income without taking on the risks of going full throttle into the world of working for yourself." Workers who aren't ready to become full-time entrepreneurs can use this technique to create additional revenue. Sometimes, diversifying revenue gives workers an enhanced sense of financial security.

As workplaces evolve, a wider range of work schedules become possible. This is helpful to those transitioning from one career phase to the next.

2
Will the Work-at-Home Life Work for You?

Only you know if working from home is right for you. There's a lot to consider, both positive and negative. As part of my work-from-home survey, I asked respondents to reflect on their own experiences. They shared the pros and cons about their work-at-home lives.

As with the reasons for wanting to work at home, I found numerous common themes. However, perspectives varied on similar topics. For example, some people rejoiced that they could prepare healthy lunches at home. Meanwhile, others saw the proximity to the kitchen as a pain point with too many snacks close at hand! Let's look at the joys and pain points you might experience.

1. Transportation

No more commuting is widely considered a perk of working from home. Avoiding the hassles of traffic jams, vehicle breakdowns, crowded commuter trains , and the general jostle of moving people around is a welcome change. You may start your work day in a more relaxed state when you work without the stress of commuting. On the other hand, you may miss the routines of commuting that aid the transition from home to work and home again.

2. Productivity

Working at home gives you the choice about when to work and when not to work. Similarly, you're in charge of how you work — at a desk, on the couch, in a café. However, this freedom requires you to use (or develop) time management and task-management skills to ensure that your work gets done. Many first-time work-at-home employees and entrepreneurs end up on a steep learning curve as they take on full responsibility for their own task lists and scheduling for the first time. This challenge can be compounded if you work with colleagues in other time zones. Depending on their schedules, you may have to work evenings, nights, or weekends to fit into their availability. Further, you must learn to overcome the boredom that comes from being in the same, monotonous space for work and home.

3. Distractions

If you've seen the Pixar movie *UP!*, you'll know how distracting a squirrel can be. Working at home is filled with potential squirrels to derail your work day. You may have trouble resisting recreational activities as you procrastinate on the work required. The temptations of binge watching a new series on Netflix, organizing your closet, or the lure of your kitchen to do what Kim Plumley dubbed "procrastibaking" could prevent you from doing your work. Crafts with your children and cuddles with your cat can also make you forget your to-do list.

Outside distractions are also a problem. You may have noisy neighbors who stomp around with heavy shoes or stream their favorite playlist at top volume all day long. Home maintenance activities such as lawn mowing, leaf blowing, pressure washing, and so on can interrupt your best intentioned train of thought. Children playing street hockey, hide and seek, or Nerf wars are equally distractions beyond your control.

Then you have to contend with interruptions from family members or housemates who assume you can be interrupted because you are home. For example, your spouse wants to discuss the menu plan, your child desperately needs to show you their teddy bear's (fake) injury, or your roommate picks office hours to cry on your shoulder over their failed romance.

4. Boundaries and Transitions

Working at home means there is no separation or distinction between home and work unless you create it. While home is always present and ready to distract you, work is constantly vying for your attention and something you should do, even after hours. Without clearly established boundaries, it's tempting to do tasks during your off hours.

Another difficulty you may encounter is how to turn off your work brain at the end of the work day. You will need to create structure to shift your mind into at-home mode. In Chapter 12, you'll find ways to ease these home-to-work-back-to-home transitions.

5. Personal Needs

A home office lets you create a lifestyle that supports healthy choices aligned with your desires for nutrition, fitness, rest, mental wellness, and so on. You can schedule naps, if that's what you need.

In addition, you're in charge of your own comfort. You get to set the office temperature, pick your desk chair, set up ergonomic computer equipment, and use your favorite coffee mug. You even get your preferred personal care supplies in the bathroom. Huzzah!

However, your home office environmental controls are limited to your home's heating and cooling systems. It's improbable that your home is equipped with an industrial HVAC system to maintain a steady 21°C/70°F. If you're spending all day in your home, do you need to upgrade your furnace or invest in air conditioning to be comfortable year round?

6. Meals and Refreshments

With your kitchen just down the hall, you have easy access to beverages, meals, and snacks throughout the day. Will you use that access to plan and consume healthy refreshments? Or will you be tempted to eat only treats and convenience foods that aren't as good for your body? Even if you're committed to mostly healthy choices, overeating is a risk when the kitchen is close at hand. And you may miss the espresso roast from your favorite coffee shop near the office.

Your break times can give you the opportunity to enjoy lunch on your patio or in your garden, weather permitting. At your discretion, you can share those relaxing coffee breaks and lunchtimes with family members or roommates.

7. Health and Wellness

Beyond nutrition, other aspects of your health and wellness can benefit from you working at home. Most importantly, you are less likely to fall ill from the office flu and other ailments due to crowded conditions, poor ventilation, and/or colleagues who won't take a sick day when they should. Reduced stress means your immune system is under less pressure and you can spend your energy doing your job.

8. Fitness

On the flip side, your body may miss the exercise you get walking to and from the bus stop, around the office, and out to lunch. You may also miss out on the opportunity to go to the company's workout room or other fitness facilities. Make sure to replace that with increased fitness activities in other parts of your life.

Happily, working at home gives you the chance to use your home gym or complete workouts at non-peak times thus avoiding crowds at the gym, swimming pool, or on walking trails.

Similarly, you also have more flexibility to fit in outdoor workouts when the weather is favorable. For example, running in Vancouver when the rain lets up!

9. Wardrobe

While you still want to look professional and presentable, as suits your job, work attire at home tends to be more casual in style and, often, more comfortable to wear. No more high heels, tight belts, or heavy blazers! Some workers choose to spend their time in pajamas, yoga gear, or other relaxed clothing. Others are less casual in collared shirts and jeans. A lot of business attire can feel too fussy and formal outside the office.

Of course, if you love fashion and have built up a substantial wardrobe of business attire — suits, dresses, handbags, briefcases, jewelry, etc. — you may look for reasons to wear your investment wardrobe.

10. Savings and Expenses

Money matters when you work at home because you'll save on some items and spend on others. Without a commute, you'll save money on transit tickets, car expenses, work clothes, meals in restaurants, and so on. However, you'll also spend money on office furniture, technology, desk supplies, and more.

11. Household Needs

You may join the ranks of those I surveyed in your glee that it is easier to take care of household tasks while you work at home. Suddenly, you have the ability to schedule appointments such as car maintenance, dental cleanings, and school pick-up during business hours. You can also run errands such as grocery shopping and pharmacy pick-ups at non-peak times. Further, you can use your break time to complete household chores. It doesn't take long to run the dishwasher, do a load of laundry, clean the toilets , etc. As an added perk, if household chores can fit into your work days, you'll have more free time during evenings and weekends because many household chores have been taken care of — at least until the next load of dishes or laundry.

12. Family Needs

You may welcome the flexibility to support family members, as needed. It becomes easier to accommodate daycare or school closures for professional development or school holidays. Similarly, it is easier to care for your sick or injured child at home. It also affords you time to help elders with grocery shopping, doctors' appointments, and social outings during the day. Additionally, you can adapt your work hours to support an ill or differently abled family member. Of course, all this family help necessitates strong productivity skills to ensure your work gets done, as well.

On the negative side, you may experience conflict with your spouse, children, or roommates if you all happen to be working (or studying, or something else) at home.

13. Professional Opportunities

Remote work may create the chance for you to work with a company you admire that's headquartered elsewhere in the world. In doing so, you could gain international experience without having to relocate.

Moreover, if you're using a remote work set-up, then you have the opportunity to be involved in projects at multiple geographic locations, not just the office that hired you. This can be a fulfilling professional experience that helps you build your network, learn new skills, and contribute to a wider range of meaningful projects.

14. Communications

Effective communication takes a concerted effort when workers are in different locations. This can be frustrating when more planning is needed to consult with employees or colleagues on minor issues. Rather than simply stopping by their desk, you have to draft an email or set up a meeting, both of which require more prep time.

At the same time, if you have a supervisor or manager, they need to make sure there are no lapses in communication to home-based workers such as you. Communication breakdowns can happen when formal updates are not communicated to all employees by email or memo. Additionally, the at-home workers may miss out on informal updates from "water cooler chat" during breaks.

Even with the increased use of video chat, there is a potential reduction in effective communication without nonverbal clues like facial expressions, posture, tone of voice, etc. Video chat has become standard business practice whether you like it or not. That means you'll also deal with related fatigue after being on camera all day. See Chapter 5 for tips to make virtual meetings easier.

One more thought, if you share a home office space, consider how your calls will impact one another. As much as you trust your spouse or roommate, you won't want to divulge any confidential information accidently.

You may also experience frustrations of having to listen to every word of one another's meetings all day long. It'll feel like you've doubled your schedule — much of it overlapping! My husband and I experienced this problem when we both started to work from home full time. Our solution is a quick chat each morning to figure out the shape of day. As needed, one of us will move to another part of the house, temporarily. This helps us both work effectively and keeps us happily married, too.

15. Social Connections

Several survey respondents mentioned that they miss in-person social interaction with office colleagues. Informal knowledge of colleagues' interests, families, activities, aren't easily achieved by email and videoconference. This creates a risk of isolation and feelings of loneliness when there's no one to talk to about work or to interact with socially.

These social problems can be compounded when extroverts and introverts work together. And you know that happens in pretty much every workplace! Extroverted colleagues use their naturally gregarious ways to join in the social fabric at the office. Meanwhile, introverted colleagues may shy away from social sharing and informal connections. That dichotomy makes it even harder for teams to maintain social connections equally through virtual connections.

As much as you're able, help foster an inclusive communications culture. Create smaller, quieter opportunities for introverts to add their voice. Be alert to the overly gregarious workers who might inadvertently monopolize the conversation. Hold space for those who need more time to gather their thoughts. Help to ensure everyone onsite and offsite are included in business-related and social messages.

16. Technical Issues

Not everyone who works at home is tech savvy and even those who know a lot about computers don't know everything. Without tech support staff onsite to assist with computer, printer, or other tech problems when they arrive, you'll have to do the troubleshooting on your own. YouTube tutorials may be your new favorite thing!

Meanwhile, residential internet access may not be as fast as internet service to commercial addresses. Further, upload and download rates may be throttled by multiple users in your home, apartment building, or neighborhood concurrently using limited bandwidth. Nothing makes your Zoom conference stutter like a teenager in the next room live streaming a video game!

One other technical area to think about is security. How will you keep the information you work with safe? In some industries (law, government, etc.) work can only be done over a virtual private network (VPN). This creates difficulties working with secure documents if only electronic access is available and print outs are forbidden.

17. Societal Perceptions

It can be a real struggle to convey to neighbors, friends, and family that you do a real job that requires your time and attention just as a conventional job does. Even if they understand, they will ask you to do favors because you're at home, not understanding that you don't have the time to take on non-work tasks.

My research also revealed that office politics are alive and well. You may experience guilt trips from in-office colleagues who question whether you're really doing any work at home. You might even suffer rude comments about the perception of being a slacker if you take your allotted coffee and lunch breaks.

Depending on the corporate culture, you may be excluded from team building and social activities offered to in-office employees. This can create feelings of in-group / out-group social awkwardness and make the work-from-home staff feel like second class citizens.

If you're considering work from home, use the Self-Assessment in Sample 1 to assess your reasons. You'll find a blank copy of the worksheet on the downloadable forms kit. You can access the kit using the web link at the back of this book. The kit includes the samples from the book as well as resources for your working from home journey.

Sample 1
Self-Assessment

Name: _Gail_   Date: _October 20_

Employment opportunities	Family obligations
• accept promotion • work with Calgary office, remotely	• before and after school care
Medical • avoid office flu	**Financial** • save on transit • decrease latte budget
Job perks • flexible hours • can still attend professional development sessions	**Other thoughts** • healthier lunches at home • time to work out • kid distractions

Sample 1 – Continued

Rate the following topics on a scale of (1) not important to (10) extremely important.

	1	2	3	4	5	6	7	8	9	10
Transportation	[ ]	[ ]	[ ]	[ ]	[ ]	[ ]	[ ]	[X]	[ ]	[ ]
Productivity	[ ]	[ ]	[ ]	[ ]	[ ]	[ ]	[X]	[ ]	[ ]	[ ]
Distractions	[ ]	[ ]	[ ]	[ ]	[ ]	[ ]	[X]	[ ]	[ ]	[ ]
Boundaries and Transitions	[ ]	[ ]	[ ]	[ ]	[ ]	[ ]	[ ]	[ ]	[X]	[ ]
Personal Needs	[ ]	[ ]	[ ]	[ ]	[ ]	[X]	[ ]	[ ]	[ ]	[ ]
Meals and Refreshments	[ ]	[ ]	[ ]	[ ]	[X]	[ ]	[ ]	[ ]	[ ]	[ ]
Health and Wellness	[ ]	[ ]	[ ]	[ ]	[ ]	[X]	[ ]	[ ]	[ ]	[ ]
Fitness	[ ]	[ ]	[ ]	[ ]	[ ]	[ ]	[X]	[ ]	[ ]	[ ]
Wardrobe	[X]	[ ]	[ ]	[ ]	[ ]	[ ]	[ ]	[ ]	[ ]	[ ]
Savings and Expenses	[ ]	[ ]	[ ]	[ ]	[ ]	[ ]	[ ]	[ ]	[X]	[ ]
Household Needs	[ ]	[ ]	[ ]	[ ]	[ ]	[ ]	[ ]	[X]	[ ]	[ ]
Family Needs	[ ]	[ ]	[ ]	[ ]	[ ]	[ ]	[ ]	[X]	[ ]	[ ]
Professional Opportunities	[ ]	[ ]	[ ]	[ ]	[ ]	[ ]	[X]	[ ]	[ ]	[ ]
Communications	[ ]	[ ]	[ ]	[ ]	[X]	[ ]	[ ]	[ ]	[ ]	[ ]
Social Connections	[ ]	[ ]	[X]	[ ]	[ ]	[ ]	[ ]	[ ]	[ ]	[ ]
Technical Issues	[ ]	[ ]	[ ]	[X]	[ ]	[ ]	[ ]	[ ]	[ ]	[ ]
Social Perceptions	[ ]	[ ]	[ ]	[ ]	[X]	[ ]	[ ]	[ ]	[ ]	[ ]

Section 2
Let's Be Practical

If you're working from home, it's important to set yourself up for success. In order to do that, there are numerous practical decisions to make. You'll need to configure your workspace, organize your meeting space, and sort out your technology needs. Those decisions include everything from ergonomic furniture to software subscriptions.

In addition, you'll also want to have the resources you need to do your work. No matter your industry, communication is vital so you'll need to ensure speedy internet access and a business phone number. You may also need safety equipment and security upgrades.

While you're thinking about the practical things, don't forget money matters such as bookkeeping, taxes, and related business finances. Those decisions tie into other resources like time management, staff, and business travel. And remember the right clothes for the job.

With so many practical considerations, it can feel overwhelming but I'm confident you can tackle each set of decisions one by one. Before you know it, these tasks will be done and you can focus on your work. Let's dive in.

3
Workspace

No matter what kind of work you do, you need some space to get things done. From tiny studio apartments to giant single-family homes, people are finding a niche to work. A corner of the living room, a converted spare bedroom, a garden shack, or a basement lair, there's no end to the potential locations. Sometimes, the chosen space is a matter of quick convenience and, sometimes, a more strategic workspace is required to get the job done.

Maybe you'd like to work from the tropics?

Nova Scotia Business Inc. launched a campaign to entice remote workers to relocate to the province of Nova Scotia. As the province's business development agency, the campaign reminded workers, "If you can work from anywhere, work from here." With affordable coastal living and innumerable nature adventures, the province has a lot to offer. Using a combination of paid advertising, social media content, and media interviews, it's an appealing offer for workers from around the world. As HalifaxToday.ca reported, ("Work-from-home campaign sees thousands interested in moving to Nova Scotia," March 21, 2021), more than half a million workers considered the opportunity in the first few months of this ongoing campaign.

In this chapter, you'll read about many factors to consider when setting up your home office. Some will be vitally important to the kind of work you do each day. Others will be irrelevant. In some cases, an offsite solution, like a rented warehouse, might fulfill your needs. Consider all the options and then organize your workspace to suit what you need most.

1. A Room of One's Own?

In her 1929 book, *A Room of One's Own*, British writer Virginia Woolf observed that, "a woman must have money and a room of her own if she is to write … " Setting gender politics aside, this sentiment applies equally to everyone working at home a century later. Some sort of designated workspace ensures that you will have a place for the technology, equipment, and supplies, as well as the mental space you need at hand.

For some, a designated room makes sense as you establish a home office. With a door to close, this is the simplest way to create boundaries, in this case a literal boundary, between work and home. (We'll talk more about boundaries in Chapter 12.) For others, a full room isn't possible but you can still carve out a designated workspace with a desk, divider, or spike tape on the floor.

In some cases, the workspace is transient as the available space morphs over the course of a day. These workers create space by virtue of the tools they arrange in any available space — often a computer, mobile phone, notebook, and related peripherals. That transient space might move multiple times each day, from bed to couch to coffee shop to dining table.

Curious how your work fits into these options? Read on to learn about some real life examples:

- Canadian food writer Rebecca Coleman moves from writing desk to kitchen to food photography set-up in her apartment over the course of each day. She's consistently developing new recipes for her next cookbook and her blog, Cooking By Laptop.

- Photographer Wendy Dphoto has inhabited various live-work studios in Vancouver. She shared, "right now my 'office' is in my bedroom and the studio is in the garage. I would love to get my office out of the bedroom. I could work in the studio/garage but there are no windows … Once the weather warms up I can work in the studio space again with the door open [for natural light]. I can't wait."

- As another example, Sue Edworthy is a highly respected marketing professional in Toronto's arts and culture scene. She works at home and spends "two or three days [each week]" at a local coffee shop she calls her "satellite office."

Whatever your circumstances, the most important thing is to understand where you will do your work and set it up so that you can succeed with whatever tasks you take on.

Interestingly, spending some time working from a coffee shop might improve your productivity. "There are many ways coffee shops trigger our creativity in a way offices and homes don't. Research shows that the stimuli in these places make them effective environments to work; the combination of noise, casual crowds and visual variety can give us just the right amount of distraction to help us be our sharpest and most creative," writes Bryan Lufkin ("Why you're more creative in coffee shops," BBC.com, January 20, 2021).

2. Environment Design

Working professionals spend huge amounts of time in their workspace. Its design should be ergonomic, functional, and, hopefully, inspiring. If your at-home workspace travels through cyberspace on video chat, you'll also want to consider the aesthetics to enhance your brand image and protect your personal privacy.

2.1 Ergonomics

First, let's consider ergonomics: the science that adapts spaces and items for your well-being. This is important because the more comfortable you are, the more productive you'll be. Plus, nobody wants a repetitive stress injury from working in an ill-fitting desk set-up. Let's avoid losing productivity because of injury!

Most everyone works at a computer, at least part of the time, so let's look at the ergonomics of computer use. The best placement for your computer, monitor, mouse, and keyboard are determined by your physical size and, potentially, by any preexisting injuries.

Consider your chair:

- Is it big enough for your frame?

- Can you sit with your feet flat on the floor while your knees are at a 90-degree angle?

- Does the backrest provide you with lumbar support? Neck support? Head support? Decide what's most comfortable for you.

- Is the seat padded to cushion your backside during long computer sessions or endless videoconference meetings?

- If the chair is on wheels, can you roll the chair easily? If not, consider adding a mat under your desk or redecorating with tile, laminate, or hardwood floors. Bonus tip: You can buy special chair wheels that won't damage your floor.

Next, position your computer monitor carefully:

- Is your monitor directly in front of you? If not, try to reposition it so you won't have to twist your neck or torso.

- Is the top of your monitor at eye level when you are seated? If not, raise the monitor to this height. If your monitor's stand doesn't reach high enough, add sturdy books or boxes underneath to reach eye level.

- Is the monitor roughly arm's length away from you? It should be close enough to see clearly but not too close.

Then, place your keyboard:

- It should be on a flat surface directly in front of you. If your desk isn't level, shim your keyboard (or your desk!) to make it level.

- Can you rest your fingers on the keys with your elbows at a 90 degree angle?

- Are your wrists straight? If they bend up toward the ceiling or down to the floor, you risk a repetitive strain injury. This can also happen if your wrists are torqued to left or right.

- If needed, consider a split keyboard (or another adaptive model). Sometimes a wrist rest is useful, too.

Finally, where's your mouse?

- Is your mouse positioned on a smooth surface?

- Is it within easy reach of the left or right side of your keyboard? Make sure to place it on the side of your dominant hand for easy access.

- Does the mouse roll smoothly? If it includes a trackball, check for dust and debris periodically. If it's an optical mouse, make sure the sensor is clean (especially after any coffee spills!)

While most businesses use computers, not all workers do everything on the computer. If you stand at a table, move supplies around, or some other set-up, take time to ensure your workspace is as ergonomic as you can make it.

2.2 Lighting (and vision care)

Lighting plays a critical role in your working environment. While it's good to see what you're doing, the right light can also bolster your mood and your productivity.

When I first set up my home office, I started with a $10 IKEA lamp which served me well for more than a decade. More recently, I've upgraded my office lights with a professional lamp from DRA-CAST. This light allows me to adjust the color temperature from warm to cool with ten dimmer settings. I've also got a west-facing window that runs the width of the room giving me lots of natural light all day long. Of course, that western exposure shines a bit too much light when the summer sun is setting so I'm glad to have blinds on the windows, too.

Typically, you'll want some general lighting to illuminate the room. Your space may already have an overhead light or, perhaps, you've installed floor lamps to bounce light off the ceiling.

Next, you'll want task lighting to brighten up your desk or any other work surfaces you use regularly. A small desk lamp or two will serve most people well.

If you're likely to be recording videos or doing a lot of video chats, you'll want to make sure you can illuminate yourself or whoever else is on camera. Ring lights are popular for this purpose as they are an easy way to direct light wherever you want it. You may also want a ground-level light behind your chair to create depth in your video shots.

If you're doing product shots, a light box will be helpful.

Still more light will infuse your office through the devices you use. Your computer monitor, tablet, and mobile phone all add to this illumination. Be aware of the impacts of prolonged exposure to the blue light emitted by your devices. Blue light can disrupt circadian rhythms, impact your sleep, fatigue your eyes, and lead to more complex medical impacts. (Read more from Harvard Medical School: www.health. harvard.edu/staying-healthy/blue-light-has-a-dark-side.) When possible, adjust your monitors to reduce blue light and consider wearing eyeglasses that filter blue light.

Sunlight is a glorious mood booster and the single biggest light we can use. While catching some rays can mean energy savings, it can also dazzle us to the point of productivity zero. If you're lucky enough to have a window in your home office space, invest in curtains or blinds so you can enjoy the benefits of natural light without squinting into the sun all day.

2.3 Interior Design

Take time to create a functional and beautiful space using whatever resources you have available. The look and feel of your workspace may simply use your existing home decor. If time and budget allows, you may want to consider interior design choices specifically for your work-from-home office. Maybe you'll hire an interior designer (or get help from a DIY savvy friend) to help you transform your space.

Working in a space that appeals to you aesthetically will support you in intangible ways. If you love your space, you're more likely to spend time there thus increasing productivity. If you're inspired by your space, you'll bolster your creativity. If you feel calm and at ease in your space, you reduce your stress and support your mental wellness.

Author, coach, and consultant Vicki McLeod shared, "In latter years I became much more intentional about the design of workspace and schedule design. I think it would have helped me manage the early stresses of a new business had I devoted more time to ensuring I had a beautiful, workable space. My first [home office] was in a spare bedroom, which was certainly adequate but didn't really inspire me. Even a few uplifting touches, fresh flowers, good art, quality supplies, make all the difference. Today I am really fussy about [my] space and it takes priority."

As you make plans for your new office, use the Workspace Design Considerations worksheet as shown in Sample 2 (available on the downloadable forms kit) to document your plans. It includes space to note the things that are important to you, your design choices, and/or office dreams. This resource also includes a layout grid and typical home office furniture icons. If you like, print out the grid and furniture to lay out your office setup without having to hurt yourself moving furniture around before you're settled on how to arrange the space.

2.4 Sound

When you set up your workspace, think about how sound might affect you and your work. Do you like to work in a quiet area? Or do you prefer some hubbub around you? Your preference may influence where you set up your home office.

If you have location options, think about whether you want to be near windows next to street traffic noises or if you'd prefer to hear children playing in the backyard, if you have one. Even in an apartment setting, you might not want to listen to your neighbors' noises. Do the people upstairs walk across loud kitchen tiles? Or is your next door neighbor's bathroom going to add flushing sounds to your home office when your home office is in the walk-in closet? It might be annoying to hear these all day and, potentially embarrassing if there's an ill-timed flush while you're on a conference call.

Some ambient noise is inevitable. Even the quietest homes include the hum of the refrigerator or the rumble of the garage door. You will have to decide how much ambient noise works for you. If you want more consistent noise, try streaming a well-known television series on low volume, playing music, or running a white noise app.

If you need absolute silence to do your work, then invest in soundproofing gear. If money is tight, soft furnishings can help. If budget allows, invest in acoustic tiles or soundproof baffles to soften the noise in your space.

Sample 2
Workspace Design Considerations

Name: _Gail_   Date: _October 26_

Space	Ergonomics
• repurpose spare bedroom • bring up desk from basement	• elevate computer monitor • purchase adjustable height chair
Light	**Sound**
• buy ring light • fix blinds to direct sunlight	• talk to neighbors about lawn mowing noise • buy sound baffles
Design	**Accessibility**
• sleek, minimalist • gray, taupe, mauve • consider video chat background	• check for tripping hazards

Make notes on what is important to you about your workspace design.

Sample 2 – Continued

Use the grid below to plan, scale, and lay out your workspace. Depending on your actual office measurements, you may decide that each square measures 30 centimeters / 12 inches, or whatever measurement works for your space. Then, you can either cut out the sample furniture and move it around the space to see how it might fit, or draw your own furniture to scale and better understand how to use your space efficiently. This is just an example of the types of furniture and space you may be working with; the best way to handle this is to work with your own specific measurements.

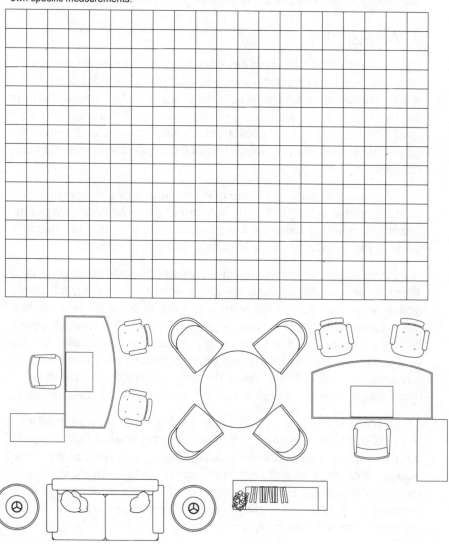

Of course, our best efforts with sound are at the mercy of unpredictable noises. We all live with unexpected sounds. Sometimes, rare noises like a search and rescue helicopter flying low overhead or a first responder vehicle with sirens blazing catch our attention. More typically, unexpected noises come from roommates, spouses, children, and pets. Managing the human (and pet!) noise is about managing boundaries. We'll talk more about that in Chapter 12.

3. Accessibility

If you require accommodations or are likely to have home-office visitors who need accommodations, you must think about accessibility when you set up your workspace. In this context, accommodations are the adjustments we make to ensure that our office is accessible to all. Whether someone uses a wheelchair or is visually impaired, careful forethought can prevent lots of frustration and, worse, harmful accidents.

Of course, if you work alone in your home office and you require accommodations, you'll already be planning around your own needs. You might need a hardwood floor to minimize tripping hazards or a magnifying monitor to be able to read computer output.

Planning accommodations for future unknown visitors is trickier. Think, in general, about mobility. Ask yourself: What are the hazards or barriers for a person with impaired mobility? Are there uneven paving stones, door jams, rugs, or general clutter that create tripping hazards? Can a person in a wheelchair enter the office easily? Should you put the office on the ground floor so that visitors don't have to navigate the stairs? What about the restroom facilities? Do they include securely fastened grab bars? And so on, it's a lot to think through.

In truth, many home offices aren't set up with accommodations in mind until there is an urgent need. Be prepared to make adjustments to make your workspace accessible to a new employee, colleague, or client, who will visit your location. Alternatively, your contingency plan might be to meet them offsite in a mutually accessible location such as a coffee shop, co-working space, corporate board room, or commercial office.

4. Hot Desks and Co-working Spaces

Both employees and entrepreneurs may have access to shared desk space at their corporate office if one exists, or a co-working space. These unassigned desks are often called hot desks and can be booked for temporary use by any eligible employee or co-working space member.

Typically, there are fewer desks than there are workers as not everyone uses the space at the same time. On crowded days, you may have to share a desk or decide to work somewhere else.

Matt Stewart is the Community Manager for Staples Studio, a co-working space in Kelowna, BC. Business professionals, entrepreneurs, and students all gather to work in this shared space. Single desks, shared desks, meeting tables, private offices, and a livestream-equipped studio theater with raked seating are available for rent. Matt shares, "You can work from anywhere. You don't need an office space but people crave connection. A co-working space can provide that sense of community without the office politics." Workers pay a fee to make use of the space that suits their needs and, as an added bonus, be part of a business community. See https://studio.staples.ca/studio/kelowna.

5. Meeting Space

While many of us work alone at our desks most of the time, it's sometimes helpful to have a face-to-face conversation with a colleague or host a larger team meeting. Depending on your home office design, you may need meeting space, permanently or temporarily.

5.1 When you need more space

Your workspace should be big enough for your everyday work tasks. When you design your home office, you'll make decisions based on what's usual for you. If you work alone, you'll plan on a workspace for one. If you host a lot of meetings, your home office will also include a boardroom table, lounge area, or some other set-up for as many people as will attend.

Sometimes, those meetings require a bigger space. Do you need room for a larger work table, white boards, projector and screen, catering facilities, or something else? Visualize the kinds of meetings you'll host. Is there a monthly board meeting? Are you hosting a workshop? Do you offer your services in a group setting? You might even host a social event now and again.

If you work as an employee, your employer likely has sanctioned meeting space that can be used, as needed, and the budget to book offsite venues for bigger events like a conference or convention. They'll also have the budget for client stewardship parties and other social events in-house or offsite at a hotel, restaurant, or party venue.

If you're an entrepreneur, you'll need to source your own spaces. Coffee shops have long been used by entrepreneurs to fill these gaps for small or informal meetings. Look to co-working spaces, hotels, conference centers, community theaters, and other rentable spaces to fill your needs.

If you plan to use a coffee shop as your home office away from home, be sure to be a considerate patron. That includes taking up space for one – not taking over a table for four. Be alert to those around you. If the café is filling up after an hour or two, it might be time for you to move on to make room for other paying customers. Make sure you make a purchase; at a minimum you'll order a cup of coffee and, if you're there through meal time, order lunch as well. If gratuities are common in your community, tip the staff generously. If you frequent the same coffee shop repeatedly, get to know the staff as best you can. A friendly greeting and a little bit of banter can boost your spirits and theirs.

4
Technology

No matter what business you're in today, you're going to need some tech gear. A smart phone, a computer, and an internet connection will let you get a lot done, whether you're a rancher managing livestock or a medical office administrator updating patient records.

If you work for yourself, you are responsible for all the technology you'll use. As a business owner, most tech will be a tax write-off, so be sure to keep all receipts and consult your tax accountant. (You'll find examples of legitimate business expenses in Chapter 9.) If you are an employee of a company or government organization, your employer might provide you with equipment to use or with an allowance to purchase work-from-home gear. Other employers will assume you have a computer at home and that you're willing to use it for work.

Before you invest in too much technology, reflect on how you will use it. Do you want to be able to pick up and go with a mobile office setup? Or are you mostly going to be at your office and better able to work on a larger screen and full-size keyboard of a desktop setup? While technology infiltrates every aspect of our private lives, the way we use technology for work involves a lot more word processing and a lot less streaming Netflix.

1. Consider Your Hardware

Hardware will be a significant business investment. You might spend $750 on a smart phone or $2,000 on a computer. Of course, there are payment plans, budget-conscious options, and luxury models. Purchasing business technology is an investment in the success of your work. You'll know how much of your budget you could (or should!) spend. Then, after the initial purchases, you'll need a budget to replace outdated tech at regular intervals so you can keep working.

1.1 Computers

Your computer will be a workhorse in your office. It can hold financial records, facilitate communication, create documentation, store information, and support creativity, to name a few functions. You'll have to choose a computer that will do the work tasks you need to accomplish.

For decades now, there's been a good-natured (and sometimes hot-headed) debate among computer users to determine which type of computer is better: Apple or PC? Today, the decision is more a matter of personal choice than functionality. Both types are compatible with typical business functions like word processing, spreadsheets, databases, email, videoconferencing, and more.

However, there are still areas where one might be better than the other. In general, Apple's computers are perceived as better for graphic design and video editing. Meanwhile, PCs have the better reputation when it comes to gaming. Further, Windows-based PCs are preferred by many businesses for work that involves application development and database analysis. Importantly, some remote access tools are only available on PC. Additionally, developers might also work remotely on Linux or UNIX systems.

As you make your decision, functionality should be your top priority. Does the computer do what you need it to do? Then, decide if a suitably powerful laptop or desktop align with your workflow and budget. While laptops have become significantly more powerful in recent years, they may not be cost effective if your work requires working with large files, graphic design, or video editing. Finally, the aesthetics and kinetics (look and feel) of one type or the other might appeal to you more and that might be the deciding factor.

1.2 Mobile phones

Your phone line will be a necessary connection to your work colleagues, clients, suppliers, and others. While you can have a business land line installed in your home, it's more common today to have a cellular phone line. This allows you to take the phone wherever you go and saves the inconvenience of modifying your home with a conventional phone.

Again, you have choices when buying your next mobile phone. The industry leaders are Apple's iPhone and Google's Android. You might choose an iPhone to better integrate with your Apple computer or, maybe, you pick an Android device to align with the models your colleagues are using.

When you pick your next phone, consider these functions to help you make the best possible choice:

- **Affordability:** How much can you spend on your mobile phone? In general, iPhones are more expensive than Android phones and you're more likely to find an inexpensive Android model if money is tight. However, you might want to splurge to get iOS features.

- **Call quality:** If you'll be using your phone to take calls, make sure the hardware is up to the task. If possible, test the quality of the microphone and speaker to see if voice calls are crystal clear.

- **Battery life:** Find out how long the battery will last and how quickly it will charge. If you're at your desk with power nearby, battery life is less of an issue but it can be annoying if you're constantly having to switch to low power mode or, worse, be unavailable by phone.

- **Apps:** Both platforms offer millions of apps but what apps will you use in your work? If you work for a medical clinic, your office's telehealth app should function on your mobile phone. Some apps, like Signal, are equally functional on both devices while others, like Pages, are iPhone only.

- **Camera:** If you'll be taking photos, recording videos, live streaming, or video chatting, you'll want to pick the phone with the best camera. Look at the specs for resolution, light, self-timer, and so on.

- **Maps:** If you'll be using maps to help you get around on the job, you'll want to compare the interface for Apple Maps versus Google Maps. Which one helps you navigate?

- **Operating system:** Apple frequently updates iOS, the iPhone operating system so users have the latest security and functionality. Meanwhile, Android phones work on various versions of the Android operating system. Be cautious when buying an Android phone to ensure it's running the latest or, at least, a recent version of Android OS.

- **Accessibility:** If you need accommodations to use your phone effectively, consider Android's easy mode to simplify phone features or rely on iPhone's accessibility customizations such as multitouch, voice, and more. iPhone can connect directly to some models of hearing aids, too, while Android phones require a gadget.

1.3 Cameras

Happily, today's mobile phones are equipped with excellent front-facing and rear-facing cameras. Many workers will rely solely on their mobile phone to take photographs and shoot videos. However, your work may require higher quality images and audio. If that's the case, you'll want to invest in a digital single lens reflex (DSLR) camera.

If you're shopping for a DSLR, it's all about how much control you have over the ways the camera handles light. Consider these factors:

- **Purpose:** What do you plan to do with the camera? Shoot still images or make videos? Are you doing food photography or action shots at a corporate event?

- **Lenses:** DSLR cameras allow you to change the lens giving you more options when it comes time to frame your next shot.

- **Image quality:** The bigger the sensor, the more data there is in the image file. That data gives you higher image quality and, in turn, more options to use the photograph.

- **Focus:** The ability to pick a focal point (e.g., a tree in the distance) and then frame your image, allows you to have more artistic control in the composition of your photographs.

- **Shutter speed:** How rapidly can you take photographs?

- **Amateur or professional:** DSLRs are available from many manufacturers: Nikon, Canon, and more. Within each brand, there are a range of cameras from beginner to intermediate to advanced. Typically, the more advanced the camera, the higher the price point.

- **Budget:** How much can you afford to spend?

1.4 Peripherals

Your technology spending isn't complete until you've picked up any needed peripherals. Think of these items as accessories that help you make full use of your computer, mobile phone, or camera. While not required, you'll find some of these other tools handy to get the job done. Here are some ideas to add to your shopping list:

- **Headphones:** Whether you prefer earbuds or earmuff style, headphones can help you improve audio quality, enhance privacy, and reduce ambient noise. If you select a wireless headset, check to make sure it works with the software you're using. Some applications may need a specific version to work correctly. The software vendor or your company's IT support people can help you determine compatibility.

- **Microphone:** While your headphones may include a microphone, you might want to invest in a more professional mic. This will improve communication on calls and elevate your brand in recordings.

- **Webcam:** Your laptop likely includes a built-in webcam but your desktop will need this peripheral to join video conferencing. Even if you've got a camera on your laptop, you might want to upgrade to high definition (HD). Bonus tip: an external HD web cam mounted on a tripod affords a more flattering angle of your double chin and turkey neck!

- **Charging cables:** While computers and mobile phones come with charging cables, it's helpful to have extras around. Sometimes cables fail or get lost so this will reduce your stress. Also, look for longer cables to give you more distance from the power outlet while charging.

- **Portable power banks:** When we're reliant on our devices to do business, no charge in your mobile phone or a power outage impacts your productivity. Purchase a couple of power banks and keep them charged for emergency use. They're also handy when traveling!

- **Power bar with USB ports:** Whether you're at the co-working space or the airport, power outlets can be in short supply. Add a power bar to your kit so you can use one plug to power several devices at once.

- **Tripod:** If you're going to be creating videos or participating in video chats, a tripod will stabilize your mobile phone or camera. Bonus tip: This leaves your hands free to take notes or complete other tasks.

- **Mobile phone mount:** To secure your mobile phone on your tripod, invest in a tripod mount. Tablet versions are available, too.

- **Green screen:** A green curtain, green easel, or green pop-up will let you edit out the background in videos. An easy way to try this is with videoconferencing tools such as Zoom. You get to choose your virtual backgrounds.

- **External speakers:** If audio is important to you or your work, consider investing in external speakers to pump up the volume and improve sound quality. These can be doubly useful during in-person events to amplify the presentation for all to hear clearly.

- **Lights:** Light will help you capture better photographs and higher resolution videos. You can start with an inexpensive household lamp, try a ring light, or invest in studio lights.

- **Reflectors:** Sometimes light doesn't land where you need it. Reflectors help you bounce light to illuminate you, your products, or anything else you want to feature.

- **Lightbox:** If you're taking your own product shots, you'll definitely want a lightbox. This simple frame creates a light reflecting backdrop to showcase your work. If the budget is tight, make your own out of foam core from the dollar store.

- **Sound mixer:** If podcasting or other audio work is part of your job, then think about investing in a sound mixer to give you more control.

- **Projector:** While your laptop screen or computer monitor might be enough for you and one colleague to see, you'll want a projector to share your work with a larger group. If needed, pick up a projection screen, too.

While this shopping list includes universally useful peripherals, you may have industry-specific tech to buy. Science teachers, for example, might invest in USB cameras that act like the old overhead projectors as well as USB microscopes.

While I've armed you with a tech shopping list in this chapter (and it is available on the downloadable kit as well), keep in mind that you won't need everything all at once. Pick up the essential items as soon as your budget allows and then plan to add more to your collection over time. In my 12 years in business so far, I've found a pattern of one major tech purchase and three minor tech purchases each year with some big spender years now and again. Don't worry if the occasional peripheral turns out to be a dud in your workflow. They can't all be winners.

2. Don't Forget the Software

Your computer will be useless without the software to do your work. Ditto the apps on your mobile phone. Bottom line: You'll need software. Some software is available for free but the majority is sold on a license or subscription basis. Let's look at what you're going to need.

2.1 Office applications

A suite of standard office applications is a good place to start. Some people use Microsoft Office (Word, Excel, PowerPoint) or iWork (Pages, Numbers, Keynote) for word processing, spreadsheets, and presentations. Others will use Google tools including Docs, Sheets, and Slides.

Communication tools are central to every workplace. At a minimum, you'll need an email program — Outlook, Gmail, iCloud Mail, or similar. You and your team may also use a messaging app like Slack, Signal, or WhatsApp to share information. Additionally, you need a video chat tool. Some people do well with Facebook Messenger and Signal, while others rely on Skype. Software like Zoom has added features that facilitate multi-person video chat, breakout rooms, and screen sharing.

Throughout this chapter, I've mentioned specific software and applications. While I have firsthand experience with most of those mentioned, please don't consider this an exhaustive list. Consult colleagues, read industry-specific publications, and consider consumer reviews as you select the software and apps that will become part of your home office set-up.

2.2 Data storage

Beyond standard office software, you may need access to a database or cloud storage to do your work. If you are an employee, your employer will provide log-in credentials. If you're an entrepreneur, you'll need to plan for data access. Without a central office server for document sharing, you can turn to document-sharing services.

Another great use of your data storage is to keep backup copies of your hard drives. While your computer and mobile phone will have onboard data storage, it's best practice to back up that data regularly, just in case you lose your phone or ruin your computer with a spilled cup of tea.

Google Drive, iCloud, Dropbox, and OneDrive are commonly used to store backups. When set up correctly, all of these services synchronize the latest version of each document across all your devices — computer, tablet, mobile phone— as well as across your colleagues' devices in other locations, if you are file sharing.

However, in some businesses, data security or confidentiality means cloud solutions aren't possible. In these cases, you'll log into a central, secure server using a virtual private network (VPN).

2.3 Audio, video, and image editing

Depending on the work you do, you you may be called on to design graphics or edit audio/ video files. If you have limited skills, you might rely on what-you-see-is-what-you-get (WYSIWYG) solutions. To generate graphics, tools like Canva and WordSwag help you create on-brand images, infographics, and posters without graphic design training. For more robust image editing tools, turn to CorelDRAW Graphics Suite or ADOBE Creative Cloud. Look for online tutorials or training at your local college to learn how to use them to best effect.

Free tools such as Audacity and Levelator will help you edit audio files for your podcast or ebook. If budget permits, subscribe to Camtasia or similar audio-video software to capture and edit screencasts, prerecorded videos, and more.

2.4 Website and content management

If you are a business owner, or your work includes marketing tasks, you're going to need software to manage your website and other content marketing efforts.

Websites can be built on many different platforms. Some are WYSIWYG solutions such as SquareSpace and Wix. Others rely on coding to publish content which might include WordPress, Drupal, or Joomla. Some knowledge of HTML, CSS, and PHP will help you navigate these coded solutions. Alternatively, you could take my approach which is to hire someone to set up your self-hosted WordPress website and then upload content on your own through the user-friendly WordPress Dashboard.

My first book for Self-Counsel Press was *The Content Planner: A Complete Guide to Organize and Share Your Ideas Online* (Self-Counsel Press, 2017). It is for anyone who publishes online including established businesses, entrepreneurial ventures, and creative entrepreneurs such as writers, painters, and musicians. The nine-step content planning cycle will help you get your ideas online efficiently and effectively to make the most of your blog, podcast, email newsletter, video channel, social media accounts, and more.

In addition, you'll need software to manage your business's social media presence. While you can rely on the website interface or app for leading social networking sites like Facebook, Instagram, LinkedIn, TikTok, and more, it's common for businesses to subscribe to a dashboard service such as Later, MeetEdgar, Hootsuite, or similar tools. These dashboards help you schedule social media content, monitor engagement, and conduct analysis. All useful functions!

2.5 Antivirus, malware, and security software

Virtual security is no joke as seemingly endless computer viruses and malware nasties wander the internet looking for victims. If you are a remote worker, your employer will undoubtedly have plans in place to protect company data. If you're an entrepreneur, make sure you cyber-protect your work.

A **computer virus** is a piece of code normally intended to damage or destroy your data. As it destroys your work, it also propagates itself through some piece of program code running on your computer. That means you could inadvertently email it to someone else. Not good!

In turn, **malware** is an even more insidious piece of code. Malware can include viruses but it goes further. This code is intended not so much to destroy your data but, rather, to hold your data for ransom or to create potentially embarrassing situations for you by exposing personal data. Imagine if you were a clinical counselor and all your patient files were suddenly published online.

Without intending to, you might pick up malware when you visit a website. This is colloquially known as drive by malware. Another way to get infected is when you click on compromised online advertising. Rather than benign advertising, this click jacking brings the malware to your computer.

Some types of malware are so insidious you don't even have to click on the malware. Simply visit the web page and now the malware can start scraping your passwords by recording your keystrokes. This makes it easy for hackers to get into your accounts. Thankfully, some antivirus software has add-ons to protect you from scraping,

There are other security considerations, too, including **phishing**. This sneaky email tactic sends you an email with an attachment that looks like it's from someone you know. Assuming it's from that familiar person, you click on the attachment and get infected with malware.

Even worse, is **spearphishing** which is more common in corporate environments. In these cases, not only does the email appear to come from someone familiar but the sender named works in your company. Plus, the name and attached file name look precisely correct. So, naturally you open it. Further, spearphishing attacks are targeted at a specific person often someone well known where it's easy to find their email address. Once the attachment is opened and the malware is released it gets to work lifting the credentials of other colleagues to repeat the process again within the same company.

Thankfully, there are steps you can take to protect your data, your computer, and your company. By default, both Windows and Mac OS include **antivirus and antimalware** at a basic level. This protective software can be configured to more intrusive settings but many users find this inconvenient as it also blocks desired files such as new software, for example.

Windows, Mac OS, and Linux — by default — all include **firewall** software that attempts to prevent any unwanted connections to your computer over a network or via internet access. A firewall might interfere with some software you use — configuring it for a specific application might require assistant from your IT department. For an individual working on one computer it's probably safest to leave it on the default setting.

Sadly, your operating system alone won't fully protect your computer. A lot more malware, computer viruses, and other types of threatware come through **web browsers**. This requires a different approach as you can't just turn off your browser and not use it. Use your digital street smarts when browsing the internet. Don't click on sketchy links! If you don't recognize what's showing up on the screen, close the tab, close your browser, and check what you typed. Generally, be more suspicious.

Another level of protection, particularly in large corporate environments, is to use additional antivirus and antimalware. This software is installed and used in addition to the basics that come as part of Windows or Mac OS. McAfee and Norton (Symantec) are the biggest players in the corporate anti-everything space. Consult your IT professional for technical guidance or reach out to McAfee or Norton's customer service desk to ask questions.

Depending on the size of the company you might also consider hiring an organization that specializes in software designed to track what appears to be malicious behavior on corporate computers and report that back to a central IT location. Toronto-based Mandiant (www.fireeye.com/mandiant.html) is one of the biggest companies in Canada that offers this **cyber protection**. Similarly, its USA-based sibling company, FireEye (www.fireeye.com/) offers cyber protection to US businesses.

Larger companies may, also, use **virtual private network (VPN)** software which has two main benefits. First, you can connect securely to a main office and, second, it prevents anything from connecting to your computer unless it comes from the main office. You have to assume there's some kind of corporate fire wall or similar to protect the enterprise level computer and server environment.

Caution: Don't equate this kind of VPN with the type of VPN service that's intended to get around regional restrictions for services like Netflix or help your teen get around parental controls. These consumer level systems don't offer any added protection.

2.6 Industry-specific software

Some software is industry specific. The functions and case uses are uniquely suited to the business.

If you're a teacher, for example, you'll access an online teaching system. Whether you're using Google Classroom, Desire 2 Learn, Blackboard Collaborate, Moodle, or another platform, the system will have many tools built in to help you distribute learning materials and deliver lessons.

As another example, accountants and bookkeepers use Quick-Books, Sage, Freshbooks, and more to help their clients manage inventory, sales, payroll, and taxes.

3. Online Access

Working from home these days usually doesn't work without internet access. At home, you'll access the internet using whatever internet service provider (ISP) you've paid to provide you with access. Additionally, you'll have internet access using the data plan on your mobile phone service. Common Canadian providers such as Shaw, TELUS, Rogers, and Bell provide both home and mobile accounts. Bundle your accounts with a single service provider for better rates.

Talk to your ISP about upload and download speeds at your home address then test their performance with an app such as Speedtest to see if you're getting what you're paying for. Sometimes, it's worth paying for a higher level of service in order to work at home effectively. You'll quickly max out your mobile phone data plan so be sure to connect your internet-enabled devices to your home internet access. Take time to check that your at-home and mobile internet services are at the right level of data for your data needs. Higher levels of service cost more so try to calibrate to keep your expenses under control. There's no point in paying for what you don't need!

Keep in mind that your home office internet likely will be shared by those who live with you. Depending on everyone's online activities you might max out the capacity of your internet connection when you share bandwidth. This is especially true when several people are live streaming, running a remote session over a VPN, and playing an online video game at the same time. This may be another reason to increase your internet access at home. If that's already top tier service, then you'll need to negotiate with everyone sharing the connection about who does what when.

To connect multiple business sites together, including your home office, you'll need to run software on your computer that creates an encrypted tunnel between your computer and one at your place of work. This link is called a virtual private network (VPN). Your company's IT department can issue you the necessary credentials if it supports this technology (assuming you aren't the IT department; if you are, it's all on you)!

The VPN your office provides should not be confused with the prevalence of VPNs available to private citizens. The latter are used to mask your location when accessing streaming services outside your country. For example, Canadian users could "spoof" the internet in order to access US-based streaming services such as Hulu. Similarly, teens often use this type of VPN to get around family restrictions on internet use. This is a dodgy area I'll delve into another day.

Another option is a tool such as LogMeIn (www.logmein.com). If your place of business will support it, LogMeIn allows you to remotely control the computer you usually use at the office from the computer you have at home. Of course, this is a paid service. If you're self-employed this is another expense that can be a tax write-off; if employed, talk to your employer to see if they'll pay for it to support you working at home.

5
Communication

Communication is key. At a minimum, you'll need to be able to talk to your customers and clients. How are you available to them? Phone? Email? Social media? Videoconference? If you have team members, you'll also need an efficient way to stay in touch. Some teams make efficient use of email and text messages. Other teams rely on tools like Slack for multiple, concurrent conversation threads. You might also have a dedicated chat thread in Signal, Facebook Messenger, or another text-based messaging tool.

A daily or weekly conference call or video chat with your team may also be a good way to keep everyone connected. You could even dedicate a Slack topic to social chit chat. Peggy Richardson from Events Plus Management Ltd. shared that their team has a "dogs in the office" thread that's entirely photos of staff members' pets captured in funny and cute moments. Create opportunities for people to casually connect whenever possible.

1. Virtual Meetings

Virtual meetings are a key element of working together when we're physically apart. As the joke goes, some meetings could have been an email. Yet, many meetings are productive and vital to the function of your company. Meeting online can help you maintain social connections in a more personable way and prevent the potential misunderstandings of a quickly written email. They're especially useful to maintain relationships between hybrid workers who never share the same "in the office" day. Otherwise, they may never connect with one another.

Researchers at Stanford University have been investigating a phenomenon known as "Zoom fatigue." While the label mentions video-chat platform Zoom explicitly, the phenomenon occurs with all videoconferencing software. As reported by Vignesh Ramachandran for the *Stanford News* ("Stanford researchers identify four causes for 'Zoom fatigue' and their simple fixes," Stanford.edu, February 23, 2021), Professor Jeremy Bailenson's research has identified four sources of that exhaustion we feel after a prolonged video call. These include excessive amounts of close-up eye contact, negative emotional consequences to seeing yourself on screen, movement being limited in ways that are not natural, and "the cognitive load being much higher in video chats." See: https://news.stanford.edu/2021/02/23/four-causes-zoom-fatigue-solutions.

If you're involved in virtual meetings, you'll need a platform everyone involved can use; a method to schedule meetings efficiently; the flexibility to cope with everyone's learning curve; and someone to take charge to keep the meeting productive. Use these guidelines to make the most of your virtual meeting (and still like your coworkers tomorrow). You could even adopt these tips as office policy to be shared with everyone involved in your meetings. That way, the team follows the same set of guidelines for every meeting.

- Schedule a meeting time and stick to it.

- Start on time. End on time. End early, if you can.

- Make sure to invite only the people who need to be there. Don't invite everyone!

- Decide who's setting up the meeting. Someone has to organize the conference call on Zoom, Skype, Microsoft Teams, or whatever tool your group uses.

- Decide who's running the meeting. Let that chairperson lead.

- Start with a brief Indigenous territory acknowledgment. You'll find information on how to do this in Chapter 14.

- Be patient with technical glitches. Everybody has a bad day when their Wi-Fi fails or their videocamera breaks. One day, it will be your turn!

- Have an agenda. Circulate it in advance. Let people prepare their contributions so that the meeting can run efficiently. Leave a spot at the end for "other business" in case of necessary additions.

- Don't hijack the meeting. Stay on topic. The sales team doesn't need to know about human resources issues. Help the chairperson keep things on track.

- Remember to get dressed. Naked is not OK. And remember: Strapless looks naked when people can only see your head and shoulders.

- Keep the dress code in mind. Generally, work-at-home attire is more business casual.

- Add a bit of levity when appropriate. Maybe log on wearing a funny hat?

- Stay alert to your audio. Your kids' argument, dog barking, and neighbor mowing the lawn might be audible. Foster a culture of mic muting unless you're speaking and adapt to the lag time while participants toggle their mute button.

- Stay alert to your surroundings. If you're working from a bedroom office, close the ensuite bathroom door so no one has to look at your toilet.

- Don't judge other people's spaces. Not everyone has a dedicated home office with a video setup. If they're calling you from the pantry or the minivan, make sure they know that's okay.

- Get some light on your face. Sitting in the shadows makes you look like a mobster on camera. Sunlight from a window or a lamp behind your webcam can work wonders.

- Be kind. Everyone has stressful days sometimes. Kids, pets, parents, plumbers may be adding stress you don't know about.

- Don't linger. Log off when the meeting is done.

- If desired, add social time to the end of the meeting but make it clear that the official part is done and people can log off if they want to. This is a great way to foster relationships between co-workers, especially those who rarely have opportunities to see one another casually in the room.

2. Live Video

Whether your work involves a lot of virtual meetings or you frequently livestream on social media, successful live videos don't happen by accident. Consistent planning and preparation for each broadcast will help you gain confidence and give your colleagues and viewers a dependable experience. Take the time to do each task for every live video you do. With practice, these tasks will only take you a few minutes.

2.1 Start with the basics

Before you go live, find the meeting agenda or decide on your topic. The best live videos focus on a specific subject. Be clear on what you will talk about.

Decide on a location where you will record your live stream. Are you filming in your office or on location? Do you need to do a quick tidy up to make sure last night's laundry isn't in the frame? Will you be indoors or outdoors? Is the spot a public space or a private location? Do you need permission to live stream from this place?

2.2 Find your gear

Of course, you'll need your camera to broadcast your video. The best camera for the job is the one you have with you. Whether you use a DSLR or a mobile phone camera, you can go live.

Once you've found your camera, check the batteries. Know that live video uses a lot of power so try to start with a full charge. You could also charge your camera while streaming. Plug it in at the office. Use a battery on location.

Shaky video will make your audience feel seasick. To stabilize your live stream, use a tripod. My current favorite is Switchpod (switchpod.co/products/switchpod) — a tripod designed for live streaming. If you don't have a tripod handy, stabilize your camera on a sturdy surface. Just be careful it won't get knocked off and damaged!

Lighting is essential to make your live stream sparkle. Let your audience see you and the things you want to share. Natural light from the sun is flattering to everyone, and it's free! Alternatively, you can arrange any lamps you have to shine light in the right places. Or, invest in a ring light or studio lights to create a live stream set with lots of lighting options.

Bad sound will drive your audience away faster than anything else. To capture the best possible audio, invest in a quality microphone. My favorite for in-office recordings is the Blue Yeti USB microphone and I love the results for the Rode SmartLav+ microphone on location. If you don't have an external microphone, the one in your smartphone will work just fine.

Pop back to Chapter 4 for more information on technology.

2.3 Consider distractions

To improve your audio, be aware of background noise. Can you shut a window to minimize traffic sounds? Or bribe your kids with screen time for a few quiet minutes? Can you stand out of the wind so that moving air doesn't create excess noise? As much as possible, record in a quiet space.

While you live stream, you are not available. Turn off notifications on your mobile phone. Close down unnecessary apps on your computer. Let people nearby know you are in do-not-disturb mode. Tell your kids you're about to be internet famous, and when you're done, let them know you're finished.

Distractions come in many shapes and sizes. Read more about distractions and how to minimize them in Chapter 12.

2.4 Look after yourself

In my opinion, the best live videos have a realness about them. The person on camera looks and acts like the real person they are rather than an actor playing a role. That said, you'll probably want to check your appearance in the mirror. Have you got anything stuck in your teeth? Are you happy with your hair? Do you want to apply a fresh coat of lip gloss? Check your appearance to boost your confidence on camera.

Now, I'm going to sound like your mom for a minute. Do you need to pee? Do a quick bladder check and hit the restroom, if needed. There's nothing more distracting than a full bladder.

While you're live, you might get dry mouth or an unexpected cough and you won't be able to step away to get a drink or a lozenge. Hydration is key to keep your vocal cords fully operational. Take a minute to pour a glass of water, just in case. If you prefer, upgrade to coffee or a stiff drink, as suits your preference and office culture. If you really want to pay attention to the details, pick a mug that complements your location or topic.

Jump ahead to Chapter 15 for more information about social-emotional wellness, mental health, and physical fitness. Trust me: You're worth it!

2.5 Final steps before you go live

Even with all this preparation, you might need to pluck up your courage. Live video is a vulnerable activity. You're putting yourself out there in real time. Be brave. You've got this!

Never underestimate the power of a cleansing breath. Take time to breathe: Inhale then exhale and repeat. Breathing may calm your nerves and settle your mind. Use each breath to focus on what you want to say in your live stream. Use each breath to ground yourself in the here and now.

If you're live streaming on social media, you'll have the opportunity to write a brief caption describing your live video. Use this copy to entice viewers to join you in real time and to encourage them to watch the replay. Whether you're live streaming on Facebook, Instagram, TikTok, or another platform, take advantage of the opportunity to write a short description.

And now it's time to go live. This is your moment: Start your live video and share your ideas with the world. Don't forget to follow the agenda and/or stay on topic. You can do this!

3. Messaging Etiquette

Whether you're a remote worker, an entrepreneurial worker, or juggling a hybrid office life, you will spend a huge amount of time messaging colleagues, suppliers, and clients/customers. Messaging tools include email, SMS text message, Facebook Messenger, Windows Live Messenger, Slack channels, and more. Oddly, the communication age makes it harder to communicate when we have so many options.

Ideally, you and your colleagues will settle on one or two messaging systems for internal communications. You might use Slack for short updates and email for more complex topics. In turn, your work may involve communication with the public as they contact you for sales, customer service, or other questions. Ideally, you or someone from your company is available to connect with your customers using the tools that suit the customers. Unfortunately, that means the tools don't always suit you.

No matter how you're sending messages, it's a good idea to have some office guidelines about what you will and won't do. Similar to the virtual meeting guidelines above, here are some recommended rules for messaging. Again, you could share them with colleagues to foster a mutually agreed-upon messaging culture in your work together.

- Address the message to the right person or group of people. Don't create digital clutter for people who aren't part of the conversation.

- Be brief. Messaging is not the place to write an essay. Complex topics may require a meeting or a full written report.

- Remember short messages are faster for you to write and easier for the recipient to comprehend. How's that for efficiency?

- Be mindful of the time of day. If you know your colleague is working late then it might be okay to message them. However, in general, send your messages during waking working hours.

- Don't forget time zones. I can't tell you how many Toronto-based colleagues message me at 9:00 a.m. (Eastern) which is only 6:00 a.m. (Pacific) in Vancouver. My night owl self gets grumpy when this happens! (And that's partly why I now sleep with my phone in do not disturb mode. In this mode, you can identify VIPs such as your spouse, grown-up children, parents, business partner, or anyone else you deem worthy. They'll still be able to reach you, even while you're in do not disturb mode, but you won't suffer calls from just anybody outside office hours.)

- Send messages at appropriate times. Don't multitask during virtual meetings or, worse, pull out your phone during an in-person conversation. How rude!

- Be reasonable about response time. Give people the freedom to respond when it suits their schedule. Accept that messaging is no place for instant gratification.

- Avoid double-texting: the practice of sending multiple messages on the same topic without giving the recipient time to reply. A postscript is okay if it adds something new. The crime comes when you repeat the same information over and over again.

- Don't ghost. Wrap up a messaging conversation much as you would a phone conversation. Add thanks, say goodbye, and sign off when a conversation is done.

- Remember that ALL CAPS is the messaging equivalent of shouting. Don't do it.

- Reflect on your office culture before using texting abbreviations. While LOL and GTG are brief, they may come across as juvenile or, possibly, rude and dismissive.

- If you decide to use text abbreviations, try to avoid obscure ones so that colleagues don't need to run your message through a translator before understanding what you've written. 10Q NP AMA BRB AFK

- Office culture will also influence your use of emojis and GIFs. Some teams love them to add a little levity to messages while others find them childish and unnecessary.

- Watch out for autocorrect. It can be a ducking nuisance if you're not careful.

- Keep the negative news off messaging. If someone is being laid off, profits are down, or there's been a death in the family, a more personal phone call or meeting is the better way to go.

- Not everyone has experience with professional messaging. Be kind as they figure it out. Even people experienced with messaging make mistakes.

- Ensure everyone on the team has access to the messaging app and knows how to use it. It's easy to overlook whoever's missing from the conversation and suddenly they're out of the loop!

In my book, *Digital Life Skills for Youth* (Self-Counsel Press, 2019), I created a text abbreviation dictionary for parents, guardians, and teachers to decode messages from tweens and teens. I've included that dictionary in the downloadable forms kit for this book, too, to help you in your messaging communications. See the downloadable forms kit accessible through the link shared at the end of this book.

6
Hygiene, Privacy, Security, and Safety

When you work from home, it may be a surprise to realize that you're also the de facto janitorial team, safety officer, and security guard. You've got a few extra things to think about on top of your usual work and I don't mean your regular domestic responsibilities. Stay tuned: We'll look at the distractions of home and how to mitigate them in Chapter 12. Meanwhile, having a home office adds an extra layer of tasks to ensure your business day goes smoothly.

1. Health and Hygiene

With no janitorial crew to take out the recycling and sanitize the doorknobs, you'll need to break out your cleaning supplies to keep your office clean. Most likely, this will be an extension of your regular housekeeping efforts. If you resist dusting or vacuuming, you'll have to accept that your home office will be dusty!

However, if your home office will be welcoming visitors, you'll want to make sure you put some extra effort into the spaces they will see such as your entry hall, your meeting space and, possibly, your bathroom. If it helps, imagine your hypercritical mother-in-law is coming to visit and give everything a spot clean just before guests arrive.

If housekeeping isn't your favorite task and you have room in your budget, consider hiring a housekeeping service to clean your home, including your office. If you're an entrepreneur, this expense may qualify as a tax deduction for your business.

If your business involves personal care — hair styling, waxing, manicures, threading — then you'll be held to a higher standard of cleanliness. Similarly, businesses that offer medical or paramedical services — massage, acupuncture, physiotherapy, chiropractic — from a home office will be subject to public health standards of cleanliness as well as the standards of your profession's governing body.

Those standards are outlined by your local health authority. Examples of items this authority will regulate include instrument sterilization, handwashing stations, disinfection of high contact areas, handling of dangerous chemicals, and much more. Seek documentation from your local health authority; as an example, check out Public Health Ontario's "Guide to Infection Prevention and Control in Personal Service Settings." See www.publichealthontario.ca/en/health-topics/infection-prevention-control/personal-service-settings.

Depending on your business license and the work that you do, your premises may also be subject to public health inspection. Typically, these unannounced visits are a formality — if you've been following your health and hygiene requirements. If not, there's a risk your business will be required to close until you're in compliance. Needless to say, it's much less stressful to keep on top of your housekeeping!

2. Privacy: Where Are You?

If you work from home, decide whether your location will be public or private. Do people need to know where you are? If you're serving clients or customers in person, then you'll need to provide your address. But do you need to list it on your website and other marketing materials? If you're not expecting visitors, then keep your home office private. There's no reason to promote your location, which can help you keep your private life separate from your work, even though they're in the same building.

Even if you'd prefer to keep your location private, there will be some public records of your location. If you're an entrepreneur, your business license, association membership, conference registration, or other documents might reveal your location. Consider using a mailbox service such as the UPS Store as your public facing address wherever it's legal to do so. Remember: Your business license must reflect your physical location, not a post office box address.

If your business has a website, make sure the domain registration details are private otherwise your address and phone number will be added to every overseas web developer's call list. (I made this mistake. Trust me: You don't want to repeat it.) Also think about turning off geotagging if you're taking business photos with your mobile phone. Otherwise, your home office address is embedded in every image. Review Chapter 4 for a refresher on digital security, as well.

3. Home Security

While you may feel secure in your home, some additional security precautions are a good idea to ensure that your work is protected. Consider both the physical access to your space as well as data security. Any breach will cost your employer or your company time, money, and, potentially, good reputation so do everything you can to protect yourself and your work.

Start by reviewing your physical set-up. Investigate these things:

- Who has access to the building? Beyond your family members or roommates, who else has a key? Your housekeeper, maybe?

- Who has access to your office? Are you working in a space you can secure with a locked door, if necessary?

- Do you need locking desk drawers, filing cabinets, or a safe?

- Do your exterior doors and windows lock securely?

- Do you have a home alarm system? Or a video surveillance set-up? Is it monitored?

Next, consider your digital vulnerability. A determined hacker will get around any virtual roadblocks, but you can take steps to make it too much hassle for these criminals to get to your information. Incorporate these strategies:

- Keep work-related data on your work-related devices.

- Don't let others use your work computer, tablet, or mobile phone.

- Use strong passwords that include upper and lowercase letters, numbers, and symbols. If you use a password manager, salt your passwords with an additional word that you type after the password manager fills in the passwords as an added layer of security.

- Use encrypted messaging if you have access to it. That way intercepted messages will be unintelligible and, therefore, useless to anyone who reads them.

- Turn on two-factor authentication whenever possible. This can be done for devices and in software.

- Use a virtual private network (VPN) but know that it may still be vulnerable if someone hacks your home Wi-Fi.

- Invest in antivirus/antimalware software to protect your computer. Use it on all family member's computers, too, so that a hacker can't get to your laptop by breaking in through your teenager's gaming computer to access the Wi-Fi.

- Pay extra attention to securing confidential digital information. You don't want to suffer a cyberattack and be in violation of privacy law.

- Understand company policies and follow them. For example, don't email secure documents to your personal email account. If you're the business owner, ensure you have a relevant policy to protect your data. If you need a template, check out Workable's Company Data Protection Policy (resources.workable.com/data-protection-company-policy).

For more on cyber protection, see Chapter 4.

4. Fire Safety

Before you could move into your home, it was approved by fire inspectors and building code inspectors to make sure that it was safe for you to live there. However, that analysis is completed assuming the space will be used as a domestic residence — not an office, studio, or warehouse.

If you work alone at a desk, fire regulations remain the same. Your home is already equipped with smoke detectors and fire exits that meet building code. Ideally, you have one or more fire extinguishers, fire blankets, or similar quick response tools on hand. However, if your work has a bigger footprint around your home, you may need to check out the rules. For example, if you are storing flammable inventory or if you work with flammable chemicals, you may be required to add fire suppression equipment, more exits, or other requirements.

If your home office will be welcoming visitors, then you'll need to review your occupancy permit and may be subject to fire-related inspection before any applicable business license is issued or renewed. In brief, more people means you need clearly marked exits, paths of egress, an evacuation plan, defined muster point, and other elements. Learn more from the Government of British Columbia (www2.gov.bc.ca/gov/content/safety/emergency-management/ fire-safety/legislation-regulations-codes) but know that your local regional fire authority will have the say in your area.

Fire safety also ties into your insurance coverage. See Chapter 9 for information about insurance related to your work.

7
Resources: Time, Talent, and Treasure

Whether you work for a big company, a start- up, or a network sales company, there's always going to be a limited amount of resources available. To help you understand those resources, frame them in three categories: time, talent, and treasure. You'll use all three to get things done. This framework allows you to think critically about how you'll use the resources available at any given moment. Together, time, talent, and treasure form a currency worth more than just money.

I first learned about time, talent, and treasure mid-career. At the time, my job was to cultivate relationships with a nonprofit's corporate sponsors. Some of those sponsors donated volunteer hours (time). Others contributed special skills (talent). Most contributed cash (treasure). Since I started working from home, I've applied it to my work regularly. It's a helpful way to frame things to get more done.

Any type of business can adapt this framework to fit their industry, products, and services. Take, for example, Gary Jones, a real estate agent with RE/MAX Canada. As needed, Gary works from his RE/MAX office and from his home office. This hybrid set-up allows Gary to be available to his clients when needed. Gary is a talented negotiator who puts his skills to work to negotiate the best possible deal for each of his clients. To support those negotiations, he hires "a company that takes super quality pictures, videos, and floor plans to keep up with technology and what the sophisticated buyers/sellers are most interested in when looking online for properties". When he's not negotiating, Gary uses his time to build and maintain friendly relationships with past, present, and future clients by phone and in-person. Time, talent, and treasure is a helpful lens that applies to organizations of all sizes, from that of the solo entrepreneur to that of a large corporation.

1. The Time, Talent, and Treasure Trifecta

Ideally, every household, or every company has access to all the resources it needs. In practice, we all have to prioritize and plan around limited resources. Figuring out the winning combination of resources creates the perfect trifecta.

1.1 What about time?

Time is a finite commodity. We each have 86,400 seconds (that's 24 hours) to spend every day. Only a portion of that is spent working. We've also got to budget time for sleep, meals, exercise, and leisure.

The more people on your team, the more time you have. At work, the available hours vary depending on the size of your team. The solopreneur has to do it all, while a larger company will assign tasks to specific employees. A marketing coordinator might take on blog writing while a marketing intern looks after podcast editing.

If you work at home, your available time is stretched between family or other home tasks and work tasks. That juggle isn't always easy. Time limits impact us all.

I apply this framework in my everyday life. My family and I only have so many hours, so many skills, and so much money to run our household. Sometimes, our individual priorities are out of alignment. Other times, the needs of my work-from-home office conflict with family plans. As a result, how we spend our time, talents, and treasures requires some extra negotiation so we can do it all.

1.2 Who has talent?

Talent is about skills and know-how. At work, people have different talents. For example, I know how to write books while my publicist takes care of media relations. We could swap responsibilities but, instead, we divide the work according to our talents.

Sometimes tasks fall to the person with the talent even if they hate the task at hand. At work, you may have a colleague who excels at digital decluttering even though they detest file management. Work has to be done even if someone's talent means they get the dirty jobs. Of course, you could outsource some tasks by hiring people with those talents. We'll talk about more about human resources in Chapter 8.

While learning at leisure is much less stressful than learning on the job, ongoing professional development enhances the talents available to any team. Everyone can learn something new. Take courses with continuing education. Read more books. Watch tutorials on YouTube. Ask a colleague to give you a lesson.

Intermixed with hands-on skills are supporting talents. Some are technical, like those of the helpful folks in the IT department. Others are soft skills or more informal roles such as team leadership, morale boosters, or mentors. These skills show up in many different ways. They are wonderful talents to have.

1.3 Treasure hunt

As the title character in the *Jerry Maguire* movie said, "Show me the money!" Think of money as treasure.

Everything we do has a potential cost. If we take on a task ourselves, we spend money on tools to complete the task. If we're short on time to complete a task, we hire help. If we don't know how to do something, we hire more help or invest in training to learn how.

At work, investments and revenue are spent on people, services, space, and equipment. That expenditure is our outlay before we consider the costs to produce goods or services. For example, staff cost money in salaries, benefits, perks, and office space (if they don't work at home). Services are an expense as well. For example, there's no such thing as free internet so, at a minimum, you'll pay an internet service provider.

Equipment needs may be capital costs but they add up, too. Computers, software, cameras, microphones, tripods, and more are all expenses. Tools are an ongoing cost, often with a fee to pay monthly or annually. These might include a social sharing dashboard, analytics monitoring, graphic design apps, and other services.

2. Time, Talent, and Treasure Budgets

With limits on time, talent, and treasure, everyone has to think about where to spend their available resources and where to conserve.

Some things can only be obtained with cash. You've got to buy those things first.

Everyone has different talents. Play to your strengths. Learn what you can. Share what you know.

Time is finite. Spend yours to maximum effect. Don't forget rest!

3. What to Do When Resources Are Scarce

We're all short of resources sometimes. If your boss is stingy or you're bootstrapping a start-up, you know what I'm talking about.

Workwise, the size of the company influences the volume of available resources. Often, employees are asked to do extra tasks on unpaid time to fill the void. In equal measure, employees work extra unpaid hours to do a good job. Meanwhile, entrepreneurs are putting in long hours, spending their personal money, and asking friends for free favors.

Tough decisions have to be made. Sometimes, we'll compromise quality. Other times, we'll postpone a project. When needed or desired, we'll seek extra time, talent, and treasure. Whatever your situation, you'll find the resources you need or accept that some business goals can't be met at this time.

Even when resources are limited, tasks at work still need to be done. Using the time, talent, and treasure framework you can decide how best to spend the resources you have for maximum effect.

8
Human Resources and Outside Experts

The soul of any business is its people. Those human resources are the brains behind everything you do. Whether you work alone or as part of a team, the people, even if that's just you, are one of your company's biggest assets. This includes the people you hire to work inside the company as well as anyone you contract to do work with you.

As we discussed in Chapter 1, the hours you spend working at home will vary according to your situation. What you do and when might be controlled by your employer, or you might be in control of your time and tasks. You may also supervise other workers to get the job(s) done.

Supervision comes with other necessary tasks including creating and keeping employee files, discipline, and conflict resolution. Managing contractors comes with a similar list of extras covering everything from billing cycles to nondisclosure agreements. Bottom line: It takes time, energy, and finesse to work with others.

1. Employees and Contractors

Assuming your work involves other people, there are several types of hierarchical relationships. Some are supervisory, some are collaborative, while others are transactional.

If you report to a supervisor or manager, they oversee your work. They'll determine the scope of your work and establish your priorities. A good manager will also show concern for your well-being and check that you have the tools you need to do your work.

In turn, you might oversee the work of other staff members or contractors. Then it becomes your responsibility to determine what work they will do, what should be done first, and to oversee their needs in general.

Much of your work might be done with peers where neither of you have a management role. In these instances, you simply work together to collaborate on the project(s) at hand.

You'll also have transactional interactions with other human resources. Examples include the driver who picks up your secure shredding bin, the ISP tech who upgrades your Wi-Fi, and the postal worker who brings your mail. They aren't employees or contractors but they make it possible for you to do your job.

Remember: Even if you work at home, you can still hire help to support you in your work. As writer Alison Tedford shared, it's important to hire help so that you don't waste time and energy "doing things outside [your] circle of genius." That means it's okay to hire a bookkeeper, a housekeeper, or anyone else you need to free up your time to do the things you're best at.

2. Hiring Help

Every company wants to find the right person to do each job. Some positions will be easy to fill with dozens of qualified candidates vying for the work. You'll find it more difficult to fill other positions, especially if the talents required are highly skilled and rare. Whether you hire a new employee or retain a new contractor, the process is similar.

You'll begin by creating a job description or request for proposal (RFP) that outlines the scope of the role and any required credentials or experience plus salary and benefits. You might also include something about the company's culture and state your position on inclusion. (We'll get to diversity, equity, and inclusion in Chapter 14.)

Once the posting is ready, plan to share it everywhere to cast your net wide in hopes of finding the perfect person. Make use of your company's website and social media feeds, especially LinkedIn as well as industry job boards or employment websites such as Indeed or Glassdoor. Be sure to include a deadline for applications or state that the posting will remain open until the role is filled.

Once you have some applications, review them to see who best meets the criteria. If you have a surplus of applicants, you may reject some for trivial things like typos or formatting errors. Do whatever you need to do to narrow the field to a select few to interview. You might also want to search for candidates online to see if their online personas match the résumé.

Take time to interview candidates to get a better understanding of their skills and potential fit on your team. Some employers do first interviews by phone or video chat before scheduling a second round of interviews in person. Others will do all interviews face to face but with different groups of people on the interview panel each time.

As you narrow your roster of potential co-workers, you may get them to complete skills testing (e.g., typing speed) and/or check their references. Once you've made your selection, you'll make someone's day a little brighter with a job offer. Wait until your first (or second) choice candidate accepts the position before informing unsuccessful candidates that you won't be hiring them this time.

3. Employee Files

It's important to keep good records of each employee. In addition to their original application and résumé, you'll want to keep a personnel file that includes emergency contact information, disclosed medical details (in case of emergency), and other details.

Over time, the file will grow as you add performance reviews, pay raises, kudos, reprimands, and any other records. Whether you keep a digital file or a paper file, be sure to keep it secured as it contains private information.

4. Nondisclosure Agreements

If the work you are doing involves proprietary information, patient files, patents, or other company secrets, all employees and contractors should sign a nondisclosure agreement (NDA). This legal document affirms the worker's understanding of confidentiality and, typically, outlines penalties for breaches of trust. Those breaches can include disclosing information, circumventing the business to help another employer, reverse engineering, and more. To give you a better idea of what's included in an NDA, I've included a sample for your reference. You'll find a copy you can adapt in the downloadable kit. When budget allows, have a lawyer draw up a standard NDA customized for your company.

5. Using Artificial Intelligence

Much of what used to be done by humans can now be done by artificial intelligence. In her book, *You and the Internet of Things* (Self-Counsel Press, 2020), author Vicki McLeod explains voice assistants like this: "There are three common digital voice-activated systems in the marketplace today — Apple's Siri, Amazon's Alexa, and Google's Google Assistant. It is predicted that voice activation will continue to grow as new applications for these services emerge. Not only is the technology improving — voice recognition software has become more accurate, able to distinguish between individual voices and tell the difference between human voice and machine voice — but consumers are becoming more comfortable interacting with voice assistants and the artificial intelligence that governs them."

As you go through your work day, you can consult your virtual assistant for calendar events and task reminders without picking up your mobile phone or touching your computer. Further, you can have your AI helper take a memo, type up and send an email, research menus for lunch, seek out needed research, and much more. As an added bonus, as long as your cybersecurity is up to date (remember Chapter 4), you don't have to worry about your digital assistant disclosing confidential information.

6. Human Resources (HR) Management Skills

In all human interactions at work, there are human resources (HR) management skills you can put into action — even if you work for

Sample 3
Nondisclosure Agreement

Desert Luxury Consulting
1350 E Flamingo Rd,
Las Vegas, NV 89119
Telephone (702) 555-1515
Fax (702) 555-1155

MUTUAL NONDISCLOSURE AGREEMENT

The undersigned parties have agreed as follows on this date: _____

That it is in the parties' mutual interest to disclose certain proprietary and confidential information or technologies, trade secrets, market strategies, projects — both digital and traditional — which are not generally known by other persons, including but not limited to inventions, product description, documentation, customer information, pricing structures, technical specifications or data, product design, packaging concept or design, distribution channels, show concepts, and other similar information which may be disclosed between the undersigned, their agents or principles.

The undersigned parties agree:

1) To hold such information, trade secrets, and strategies in confidence and not disclose the same to any third party or use the same for competitive purpose or advantage;

2) To agree to non-circumvention of customers and/or business relationships or strategies and concepts without prior consent through written, binding instrument amended to this agreement;

3) To use such information, trade secrets and strategies only for the purpose of evaluating proposals and projects or developing projects pursuant to a written agreement authorizing the application or in the enjoyment of rights and privileges extended through this overall agreement;

4) That this agreement does not convey any rights to reserve engineer with purpose of obtaining a working model of similar product or technology;

5) Not to publish, release, disclose, or allow to be viewed or communicated in any form to any person not a party to this agreement, without the disclosing party's prior written permission; and;

6) Upon termination of discussions to return all tangible representations of such information, trade secrets, and strategies.

Disclosure of such information, trade secrets, and strategies shall not confer any rights or interest in the same.

No representations or warranties are made concerning the accuracy, validity, feasibility, or possibilities for implementation or abandonment by future actions, irrespective of provisions contained in such information, trade secrets, and strategies.

Initials: Company A:_____   Company B:_____   Page 1

Sample 3 – Continued

Either party may obtain injunctive relief in the event of breach by the other, in addition to actual damages and all other remedies available by law. The parties recognize that breach may cause irreparable injury and that damages will not provide an adequate remedy. Such action may be brought in the jurisdiction where such action is sought to be enjoined State courts located in _____.

[CITY, PROVINCE/STATE].

The agreement will be binding on the parties, their successors and assigns for the later of the period of five (5) years or the full term of the agreement to which this is attached. The obligation to protect confidentiality shall survive termination of all agreements of the parties.

The undersigned hereby enter into this Agreement on this date on behalf of the undersigned and all agents, principles, and assigns obtaining such confidential information pursuant to this Agreement.

_____   _____
Company A   Company B

_____   _____
Address   Address

_____   _____
By: By:

_____   _____
Print Name: Print Name:

_____   _____
Company: Company:

_____   _____
Title: Title:

_____   _____
Date: Date

yourself. These strategies enhance communication, streamline workflow, and ensure you and any colleagues are contributing to the best of your abilities. Consider the following:

- Give your full attention to colleagues and truly listen. Observe their body language and notice their inflection. Try to reflect your understanding to ensure mutual understanding.

- Give effective instructions that clearly outline what needs to be done. If necessary, show someone how to do a new task. Offer encouragement and praise.

- For better or for worse, accept responsibility no matter what happens. Rather than place blame, use problem-solving skills to find a workable solution.

- Look for obstacles so you can identify problems and fix them. Don't assume an employee or contractor is the source of the problem. Look deeper to see if there's a systemic or equipment issue.

- Use time wisely by setting priorities and delegating tasks. Provide a reasonable amount of time for tasks to be completed and remember that no one is productive 100 percent of the time.

- Use positive reinforcement to let people know when their performance is appreciated.

- Show people that you care about them as people, not just as workers. Show interest in their families and hobbies. Celebrate birthdays and milestones. Offer empathy when tragedy strikes.

- Communicate decisions so that team members know what's happening and why.

For more expert support with your human resources, check out the educational materials available from Charter Professionals in Human Resources Canada (cphr.ca) and the Society for Human Resource Management (www.shrm.org).

9
Finance

Whether you work for yourself or work for someone else, you're going to have one eye on the bottom line to ensure your business is profitable. If you're an employee, your project or department will be given a budget determined by management. Part of your job is to complete your work on budget or, even better, under budget. If you're an entrepreneur, you'll be in control of the entire budget and any related financial matters such as payroll, taxes, and insurance. Profitability is your goal, too.

Let's take a closer look at finances. Keep in mind that some financial information differs if you are an employee rather than an entrepreneur. And, if you're an entrepreneur, the way your business is structured — sole proprietorship, incorporation, limited liability partnership — will also influence how finances play out. I'll highlight those differences as you work your way through this chapter. Even so, many of the fundamentals are the same for all types of businesses.

If you're new to finance, I encourage you to learn more about how money works in your business. You'll feel better prepared for meetings with your accountant or financial advisor if you understand the precise terminology they use. You'll also be better informed to make business decisions on sound financial footing. For a deeper look, I recommend Angie Mohr's book *Financial Management 101: Get a Grip on Your Business Numbers* (Self-Counsel Press, 2007).

1. Budgets

As part of business planning, many companies establish an annual budget to determine their overall expenditures and anticipated revenues. While the realities of the financial year may play out differently, the budget acts as a guidepost to keep the work on track financially. Monthly reviews of progress to date determine if the company needs to make any adjustments, whether to reduce expenses, save profits, or reinvest revenue.

1.1 Revenue

All of your business efforts are focused on maximizing revenue. Collectively, all your income streams are accounts receivable; money to be paid to your business. Depending on the nature of the business, you might generate income with one or more types of revenue such as:

- The retail price of goods sold. Sell a children's toy for $14.99, and earn $14.99 in gross revenue.

- The retail price of services rendered. Sell a marketing consultation for $600, and earn $600 in gross revenue.

- Ongoing royalties for intellectual property such as books, music, and other copyrighted content.

- Crowdfunding to support your work. A service like Patreon gives your fans a chance to support your work with a monthly monetary contribution.

- Grants from all levels of government: civic, provincial or state, and federal. Grants do not have to be repaid.

- Business loans through your bank or another funding body. Loans are advantageous to help you start or grow a business. Keep in mind that loans must be repaid with interest.

Most businesses have multiple revenue streams to mitigate their risk. If one product or service sells poorly, sales of other items will sustain the business.

1.2 Expenses

On the flipside of revenue, you'll find expenses. Business expenses are the costs you spend to run your business. Collectively, they are known as accounts payable or, more, simply bills to pay. Ideally, revenues exceed expenses so your business is profitable. If the opposite is true, and expenses exceed revenues, then your business is operating at a loss, at least temporarily. Keep in mind that your business expenses can only include legitimate costs that you can write off at tax time. Sorry, that means your office LEGO isn't tax deductible, in most situations. Legitimate expenses include things such as:

For more detail on allowable business expenses, consult the Government of Canada web resources for business use of home expenses (www.canada.ca/en/revenue-agency/services/tax/businesses/topics/sole-proprietorships-partnerships/report-business-income-expenses/completing-form-t2125/business-use-home-expenses.html) or, in the United States, consult the Internal Revenue Service (IRS) https://www.irs.gov/taxtopics/tc509 for current regulations. If you're daunted by the bureaucracy, work with a professional tax accountant who knows the rules in-depth.

- **Business license:** To legally operate your business, you'll need a business licence that reflects the type of work you're doing: retail sales, consulting services, etc. Your city may offer a specific business license for home-based businesses. If you are an employee, you are not required to have a business license, in most jurisdictions. Check with city hall to confirm the requirements that apply to you.

- **Professional services:** You may need a lawyer, accountant, or other professional to help you run your business.

- **Financial costs:** You'll pay monthly bank fees, annual credit card fees, interest on loans and late payments, and other banking related costs.

- **Vehicles:** The cost of your car lease or monthly vehicle payment can be considered a business expense if you use your car for business purposes.

- **Vehicle expenses:** Add insurance, fuel receipts, and car washes plus regular maintenance and emergency repairs to your expenses. It's not cheap to run a vehicle. **Tip:** If you're using a personal vehicle for business, keep a mileage log so you can determine how often you drove for business reasons. **Bonus tip:** Note odometer readings for your vehicles on December 31 (or your company's year-end) annually so you can track business use.

- **Transportation expenses:** If you use other types of transportation, those expenses can also be business expenses. This can include public transit tickets, taxi fares, and rideshare fees. You can also use business travel expenses by train, plane, ferry, plus meals and hotels. See Chapter 10 for more on business travel.

- **Inventory:** Any expenses related to buying or manufacturing the goods and services you sell are clearly business expenses. **Tip:** You'll need a way to track your inventory. Low-volume inventory can be counted manually while high-volume inventory will be easier with digital tracking.

- **Shipping and handling:** If you're selling goods, you're going to incur shipping costs including postage, courier, packing materials, shipping labels, and so on.

- **Human resources:** If you've got people working with you, you'll have payroll for employees and invoices to pay for contractors. You'll also have fees for service providers and, let's hope, you have a little budget for staff perks. (Donut day, anyone?)

- **Location:** When you work at home, you can calculate what percentage of your home is workspace. For example, if you have a 2,000 square foot home and your office is 100 square feet then you can use 5 percent of your rent or mortgage as a business expense. You may also be able to use a portion of maintenance, landscaping, cleaning, and similar costs.

- **Utilities:** You can use a proportional amount of your utility bills as business expenses. Don't forget to save your invoices for electrical, natural gas, telecommunications (mobile & landline), internet service provider (ISP), and more.

- **Office supplies:** Everything from pens and copier paper to computers, peripherals, and other things you need to do your work are legitimate expenses.

- **Marketing:** You've got lots of options when it comes to promoting your business. All of the related expenses are eligible. Don't forget your publicist, website designer, website maintenance, web hosting, social media dashboard, advertising, analytics tools, podcast syndication service, email newsletter tool, and more.

- **Entertainment:** Meals out with clients, hosting parties, catering, performers, event staff, and more are all legitimate expenses.

- **Professional development:** Lifelong learning can be a business expense. Within limits for your tax jurisdiction, workshops, courses, conferences, and memberships can be used.

- **Business specific:** The unique tools and requirements of your business might include additional legitimate business expenses. For example, a chef can write off their knives and chef's jackets as well as cookbooks purchased as research materials.

Entrepreneurs and employees take note: You are not responsible for filling any financial shortfalls. As author Alison Tedford notes, "Your business doesn't exist to subsidize other people. It's there to sustain you." All too often employees cover necessary business expenses out of their own pockets. Entrepreneurs are guilty of the same mistake giving the illusion of a profitable business even though it's unofficially subsidized. Once upon a time, I worked in a job where my primary purpose was to build relationships with corporate executives. However, I had no budget to attend conferences, board of trade events, or chamber of commerce lunches. I had to purchase my own tickets to attend and the company reaped the financial rewards of those relationships. Learn from my experience and don't do this!

It's important to note that some expenses will change cost over time. These are called variable expenses. Imagine you are seamstress who makes custom cosplay costumes. One of your most popular designs is a version of Princess Leia's cold weather gear from *The Empire Strikes Back*. The cost of that white, puffy, quilted fabric, may change overtime depending on availability. In contrast, you also have fixed expenses that rarely change. The cost of your website hosting, for example, should only be subject to occasional increases to reflect inflation or higher levels of service.

2. Bookkeeping

Keeping track of financial transactions requires ongoing bookkeeping to record every bit of income and all expenses. Depending on the scale of the business this work might be done annually or quarterly but it's most common to do monthly bookkeeping. This allows the business to check in with financial progress and make adjustments, as needed.

In general, employees have limited involvement in bookkeeping unless they happen to work in the accounting department! You may have to submit a timesheet to ensure your paycheck reflects your work. You'll also fill in an expense form to be reimbursed for any approved out-of-pocket expense you've incurred on behalf of the company.

Bookkeeping for entrepreneurs is more complex as you'll be tracking all revenue and expenses for your entire company — no matter its scale. However, you don't have to do all the work if you hire a professional bookkeeper or certified public accountant (CPA) to work with you. Smaller companies will contract these financial services while larger companies often have in-house staff who take care of all aspects of finance.

If you're in the market to hire a bookkeeper or CPA, consider these tips to find the right person for the job:

- **Ask for referrals.** Family, friends, and colleagues enthuse about CPAs they adore and are quick to tell you about the ones who create nightmares. (I have nothing nice to say about the accountant who lied about their credentials. As it turned out, they were not a certified professional accountant. Grr.)

- **Reflect on your needs.** Is your small business staying small? Do you need an accountant who will grow with your business? Are you selling in more than one currency? Are you more comfortable working with a small office of 2 or a massive corporate office of 400?

- **Seek the right expertise.** Do you need someone who specializes in tax audits or someone who understands real estate deals?

- **Think about fit.** While you're not going to spend much social time with your bookkeeper, it's easier to work with someone if you communicate easily and share a common interest or two.

For more human resources tips, reread Chapter 8.

2.1 Statements

When bookkeeping is done well, many different reports can be generated to show you how your business is performing financially. It's a good idea to learn to read these reports so you can take action to fix small problems before they become big problems. You'll also be able to recognize the wins so you can celebrate those, too.

- A balance sheet provides a snapshot of your business' financial picture at a specific moment in time. It includes the company's current liabilities (what it owes), assets (what it owns), and equity (what is invested in the company).

- The income statement is a document that shows if a company is profitable or not during a certain period of time.

- Cash flow statement shows you how much cash (or cash equivalents) your company has available to pay bills, settle payroll, invest in new inventory, and other obligations.

In the downloadable kit, you'll find examples of a balance sheet, income statement, and cash flow statement. Don't worry, you don't have to create these spreadsheets row by row. Thankfully, accounting software such as QuickBooks generates these reports once the data has been entered.

2.2 Payroll

If you're an employee, payroll is more about ensuring your paycheck correctly reflects your salary. If you're an entrepreneur, you'll need payroll to ensure your employees are paid their salaries and your contractors are paid their fees. Payroll is also where you'll keep track of benefits like medical, dental, and other perks. In addition, payroll helps keep track of leave whether an employee is entitled to paid vacation days, takes sick leave, or is away on short-term disability or parental leave.

In addition, your payroll system will help you generate income tax slips for your employees. These must be issued annually as described by Revenue Canada, the Internal Revenue Service, and their peers in other countries.

Canadian workers will receive a T4 Statement of Remuneration Paid (www.canada.ca/en/revenue-agency/services/tax/businesses/topics/payroll/completing-filing-information-returns/t4-information-employers/t4-slip.html). Depending on the terms of their work-from-home office, they may also be entitled to a T2200 slip documenting their home office expenses. Their US counterparts will receive a W-2 Wage and Tax Statement (www.irs.gov/forms-pubs/about-form-w-2). These documents tally the income tax and other amounts deducted from each paycheck and reflect the amounts the business has submitted to the government on behalf of the worker.

3. Loans and Grants

Whether you're starting your business or growing your business, it's common to borrow money. You might need a start-up loan to launch your business idea or a government grant to pursue a project. Extra funds will also help you increase capacity, develop new products, open another location, and much more.

3.1 Loans

Of course, loans must be repaid with interest within a set period of time. Make sure the loan makes business sense so that you're not taking on more debt unnecessarily.

Let's say you run a donut shop and you can't keep up with customer demand. You might take out a $10,000 loan to renovate your commercial kitchen to increase the number of donuts you can bake each day. At 5 percent interest over 3 years, the loan will cost you $789.52 in interest. If the increased capacity allows you to earn an average of $17 more in donut profits each day, you'll profit an additional $18,615 (3 years x 365 days x $17 = $18,615 profit), much more than the cost of the loan.

The Business Development Bank of Canada (BDC) has a handy online tool that will help you calculate the cost of a loan (www.bdc. ca/en/articles-tools/entrepreneur-toolkit/financial-tools/business-loan-calculator). Use it to explore if borrowing money makes sense for your business, and then consult your banker for a more in-depth analysis.

Needing or wanting a loan does not guarantee your lender will approve the funds. Remember that they will review your overall financial position and assess your ability to service the debt (make monthly payments) on top of your business' other financial obligations.

If your business is a sole proprietorship, remember there is no legal distinction between you and your business. This means you need to ensure your personal finances are in order before you go looking for a business loan. Unpaid debt, credit card balances, and low credit scores could prevent you from growing your business.

3.2 Grants

Grants are another potential source of funds. The key difference between grants and loans is that grants don't have to be repaid. Research potential grants and consider applying for any that you are eligible for. You'll find grants to support certain kinds of work (performing arts, scientific research, etc.) and grants to support certain kinds of people (BIPOC, women, immigrants, etc.). There are seemingly endless grants available from thousands of funders — the tricky part is finding the right fit and submitting a successful application.

If you're a performing artist or do work related to music, theater, or dance check out grants from the Canada Council for the Arts (canadacouncil.ca/funding/grants), The Kennedy Center (www. kennedy-center.org/education/opportunities-for-artists/) or similar umbrella arts advocacy organizations in your area.

In contrast, businesses interested in developing export markets, can apply for grants from Economic Development Canada (edc. stlhe.ca/funding/edc-grants/), the U.S. Economic Development Administration (www.eda.gov/grants/), or similar programs in other jurisdictions.

Keep in mind that grant applications require a detailed application. In some cases, the time needed to complete the application might be worth more than the funds you'll earn from the grant.

4. Taxes

As the joke goes, two things are for certain: death and taxes. If you're in business, you'll need to deal with several types of taxes regularly.

Employees and sole proprietors will file personal income tax returns. Corporations and limited liability partnerships will file corporate taxes and produce a legally required annual report requirement.

Your company may have to collect sales taxes from your customers and clients. These fees are charged on top of the retail prices of goods and services and then remitted to the government. In Canada, we have three types of sales tax:

- Federal goods and services tax (GST)

- Provincial sales tax (PST)

- Harmonized sales tax (GST + PST)

Businesses can claim a GST rebate for GST paid on goods and services the company has purchased.

In comparison, the United States does not charge a federal sales tax but individual states are allowed to charge variable rates ranging from 0 percent in Oregon to 7 percent in Mississippi. The Sales Tax Institute maintains a list of state-by-state sales tax rates (www. salestaxinstitute.com/resources/rates) for easy reference.

Additionally, some countries, including the United Kingdom, Croatia, South Korea and many other jurisdictions charge value added tax (VAT). This surcharge adds to the cost of goods at every step of the supply chain. The United States Council for International Business shares a list of VAT rates from around the world (www.uscib. org/value-added-tax-rates-vat-by-country/).

Although you may be tempted to file your business taxes yourself, I encourage you to hire a professional tax accountant each year. The cost of filing may be an unwanted business expense, however, part of what you're paying for is your CPA's support in the event that you are selected for a tax audit. The potential stress of an audit is significantly reduced if you trust your CPA. If you're audited, suddenly that filing fee will seem like a bargain!

See the downloadable kit for a handy tax-time checklist you may decide to use in your work.

If taxes have your mind spinning, or you're about to be audited, take time to learn more. Businesses based in Canada will find Dale Barrett's *Tax Survival for Canadians* (Self-Counsel Press, 2013) informative. Concurrently, US-based businesses can read Scott Estill's *Tax This! An insider's guide to standing up to the IRS* (Self-Counsel Press, 2012).

5. Insurance

Another financial area to explore is insurance. Insurance can protect your assets and help you recover in the event of a disaster, tragedy, or legal action. There are several types of insurance to consider.

First, look at your home insurance policy. Talk to your insurance broker to inform the insurer of your home-based business activities. If necessary, add an additional rider.

Similarly, make sure any vehicles you use for business are suitably insured. If your company owns the vehicle or the lease, the company will hold the insurance policy. If you're using a personal vehicle for business, make sure you get the right level of insurance based on the number of days you use it for work. The limits are different for pleasure use, commuter use, and commercial use. Again, talk to your insurance broker.

Three other types of insurance to investigate are errors & omissions insurance (E&O), liability insurance, and critical illness insurance. Consult with your insurance broker and your lawyer to discuss the potential risks your business will face. Purchase coverage that makes sense for the goods and services you provide.

6. Business Banking and Expertise

Your business needs professional financial support. This includes the services available at a bank or credit union. Deposits, withdrawals, loans, and more all help you run your business. Your financial institution will likely offer a financial advisor to help you understand your financial position and to make business decisions. You'll work in cooperation with your accountant (who will help you do your taxes!) and your bookkeeper (who will turn all your receipts and invoices into financial statements). Together, these experts will help you plan your potential capacity, understand your breakeven point, and, perhaps, most importantly, calculate your key performance indicators (KPIs) —an important tool to determine your business's strategic, operational, and financial achievements.

10
Business Travel

Business travel is a part of many businesses. You might travel frequently to visit existing customers and build relationships with potential customers. If your company manufactures products, you might travel to visit the factory where your items are made. Travel might also be necessary to inspire your next product line as you explore a location to better understand the local culture and get to know its artisans.

Your business travel might be more mundane — a regional manager visiting all the locations in their territory or an annual team-building event at a local hotel. If you're feeling a bit James Bond-ish, perhaps, some corporate espionage could be in your future. I'm kidding, of course, but it's always a good idea to check out the competition.

Work travel creates great opportunities for key personnel and leaders from all over to come together in person. This affords potential to build relationships and foster more effective teams. As a remote worker or hybrid worker, these are valuable outings to improve your working relationship with everyone in the company's organizational chart.

When it comes to business travel you'll move your home office to your temporary home away from home. When you visit another place of business, you still have to be able to do your job, or some parts of it. Even on vacation, you might mix business and pleasure even if you are, technically, off work.

In your travels, you'll likely end up working on planes, trains, and in automobiles. Work can be a good distraction when waiting at airports, train stations, and ferry terminals. Undoubtedly, you'll also have some downtime in your hotel room. With forethought and careful planning, you can be effective and productive wherever you are.

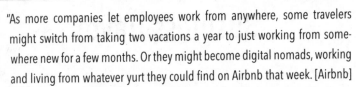

"As more companies let employees work from anywhere, some travelers might switch from taking two vacations a year to just working from somewhere new for a few months. Or they might become digital nomads, working and living from whatever yurt they could find on Airbnb that week. [Airbnb] has recently been promoting the idea of trying out a new city before moving there, for instance, now that lots of people are free to leave the immediate vicinity of their employers." ("Airbnb thinks remote work will change travel forever," Protocol. com, May 24, 2021.)

1. How Often Will You Travel?

Business travel might be a regular activity as part of your job. (Hello, frequent flyer miles!) Maybe you'll become accustomed to being away from your home office many weeks of the year and gain a lot of experience working wherever you can. Sales representatives, professional speakers, athletes, and others are likely to be on the go often.

Or, if your job does not require you to travel on a regular basis, you may still take the occasional work trip. A few times a year perhaps you'll venture out to attend meetings at head office, go to a conference, be part of an annual retreat, or be present for a quarterly product briefing. If your professional development includes in-person training you could also travel to take a course and/or go to an authorized testing center. Maybe the company you work for holds an annual summit to bring everyone together once a year for meetings and a great big party.

2. Mobile Office

As you pack your suitcase, your packing list will likely include a portable version of your office. Typically, this includes your mobile phone, computer, chargers, pens, and notebooks. You may also need peripheral items such as your tripod or battery pack. Don't forget product samples, client gifts, and swag to give away if that's part of your business model. Plus your personal items, of course!

Throughout your journey, you'll have to set up a temporary office in whatever space you can find. While your hotel room will usually have a desk, most hotels also have a business center — that can be handy if you need to print something or photocopy handouts. If you need more space or more privacy, consider booking a meeting room with the hotel's events team.

When traveling by air, you'll find spots to get some work done — both on the ground and in the air. Pull out your mobile phone to check emails, messaging apps, and social media feeds while standing in line to pass through security or sitting on an airport shuttle. Once you're more settled in the airport lounge or on your plane, it'll be easier to pop open your laptop and do more of your work. Before you fly, check to see if your plane is equipped with in-flight Wi-Fi. Also, check your bank account to see if you can afford in-flight Wi-Fi. Cha-ching! If not, download any documents you'll need in the air and be sure to back them up as soon as you have internet access again.

One more thing: Please respect and follow the flight attendants' instructions about electronic devices. Don't add drama to their stressful jobs by being the passenger who has to be asked to power down their laptop twice!

If traveling by car, you can create a mobile office on the move. But, please, don't work while driving! If you're a passenger in the vehicle or at a rest stop, you can get to work anywhere. To make your in-vehicle experience more comfortable, consider purchasing a car desk. You'll find many models on the market. Some hang over the front seats creating a work surface in the back seats while others can attach to the steering wheel or upgrade your console. Many of these are compact enough that you could take them with you on a long distance trip if you fly into a new city and then rent a car. Try not to rely on running your computer off your car battery for too long — a flat battery will make it tough to be on time to your next meeting.

Don't forget: If you're visiting a branch location or a customer's office, they might have a hot desk, spare office, or board room where you can work while you're onsite. Don't forget to book a hot desk in advance to make sure you have a space!

Wherever you travel, remember that public libraries have Wi-Fi, work tables, and, sometimes, coffee. They're usually quiet spaces to work and you've got research experts on hand, if you need their help. That's a win-win.

3. Packing List

One of the best things I created when I started traveling for business was a master packing list. Honed over many years, I reuse the same list trip after trip and it saves me lots of time. It helps me map out what clothes to pack and prevents me from over-packing. (Can you relate?) With my list in hand, I don't worry about forgetting all the little things. If it's on the list, it will make it into my bag.

You'll find a copy of my master packing list in the download kit. You're welcome to use it as is or you can adapt it to create your master list. Travel is stressful enough, let's not make it more stressful by forgetting anything essential.

See the downloadable kit for a master travel packing list you can print and reuse.

Bonus tip: I keep two versions of the list: one for when I'm traveling by car and I have room to take lots of extras and another for trips with limited luggage capacity.

4. Travel Tips

While the internet is filled with travel tips, business travel adds extra layers to the process. Here are some travel tips to help you along your journey.

Timesavers:

- While tickets and reservations are entirely digital these days, bring printouts of your tickets, boarding passes, and reservations, in case your phone runs out of power or has an unfortunate accident on the gangway.

- Splurge on higher quality luggage. Nobody has time to deal with broken zippers and wheels that fall off.

- Pack your favorite pen and notebook. You don't need the frustration of using a low-quality hotel pen and tiny hotel notepads.

- Keep your bags packed between trips. Buy toiletries, charging cables, and other things in duplicate so you've got a travel set that lives in your suitcase.

Personal comfort:

- Travel light to reduce the amount of stuff you have to schlep around airports, train stations, and hotel lobbies.

- If you fly frequently, purchase an airport lounge membership. You'll have access to a quieter place in the airport with desks and food. That's a win-win.

- If you have to go to a work meeting straight from the airport, have a change of clothes in your carry-on luggage so you can quickly refresh when you land.

- Pack some casual clothes so you can explore the places you visit as a tourist when the work is done.

- Pack things that will help you sleep. An eye mask, a pillow, melatonin, a teddy bear —whatever works for you.

- Pack some over-the-counter remedies including acetaminophen, ibuprofen, antacids, diarrhea medication, electrolyte powder, and anything else you might need, just in case. You may not feel up to finding a pharmacy in a strange city.

- Hydrate! Carry an empty water bottle through security and then fill it before you board your flight. Use the same water bottle on the nightstand in your hotel room to remind you to drink more water during your busy business days.

- Remember to eat! Tuck a few small snacks into your bag. Have groceries delivered to your hotel room. Keep your eyes open for healthy food in your travels.

- Try to sneak in some sightseeing — even if it's just a few minutes between meetings.

- Take photos with your mobile phone. Use them to document your trip: your hotel room number, the license plate on your rental car, the name of the restaurant, and as digital mementos of the people and places you visited, even if it was all work-related.

Travel days:

- Schedule travel with some buffer time so you don't exhaust yourself. Arrive early so you can walk in the park near your hotel or leave later to fit in a massage before you fly home.

- Choose nonstop flights when you can. Hopper flights and lay-overs needlessly lengthen your trip.

- Arrive at the airport (or train station) with your electronics fully charged so you can use any downtime productively or listen to a new audiobook.

- Aim to fly with carry-on luggage only. This will save you the hassles of baggage check, baggage claim, and, worst-case scenario, lost baggage. One small suitcase and one personal item is plenty for trips up to a week or more. Of course, that's assuming you don't travel with a sample case or other bulky business items.

- Use a small shopping bag to gather the items you want in your seat before you board the plane. Then you can walk on, stash your bag, and sit down without holding up the line in the aisle behind you.

- Make it easier to clear security checkpoints by having your liquids and electronics readily accessible.

Hotel:

- Make your hotel room work for you. Tuck tourist brochures and info cards into a dresser drawer then use the surfaces to spread out your personal belongings.

- Claim the desk and make the most of it. Setup your laptop and office supplies as soon as you unpack so you're ready to work anytime.

- Book a higher quality hotel that offers complimentary robes, slippers, or workout gear so you don't have to pack your own.

- Make use of the hotel lounge or coffee shop for casual meetings with colleagues.

- If budget allows, upgrade your room so you have more space to work. A room with both a sofa and a bed or a suite with a separate bedroom can make your trip more comfortable.

- If the hotel you want is fully booked for your travel dates, take a look at Expedia, Hotwire, Trivago, or other central booking services. Often one or two rooms are available through those services that shows as booked on the hotel side of the reservation system.

Loyalty programs:

- Join hotel loyalty programs. Many hotel chains offer free Wi-Fi, room upgrades, complimentary breakfast, and other enhanced amenities to their loyal customers.

- Join airline loyalty programs. Frequent flyers benefit from seat upgrades, complimentary lounge access passes, no charge in-flight refreshments, and more perks.

- Use a loyalty program credit card. Take out a VISA, MasterCard, or AMEX connected to a loyalty program. All your purchases with the card will earn you additional points. If you want to earn points on both business and personal purchases, apply for two different cards to keep work and home finances separate.

- Layer loyalty programs. It never hurts to ask what loyalty programs are connected to your travel. For example, travelers who stay with Coast Hotels can collect Coast Rewards' points and collect Aeroplan miles for every stay. Pay with your loyalty program credit card for even more points.

- Book within the same family of hotels whenever it's practical. Often multiple hotel brands share the same loyalty program. For example, the Accor Live Limitless loyalty program can be used at Fairmont, ibis, Mercure, Hyde, and other hotels and resorts.

Travel savings:

- Auto club savings. If you belong to the Canadian Automotive Association (CAA) (www.caa.ca) or the American Auto Association (AAA) (www.aaa.com), check to what discounts are currently available. You'll save on hotels, restaurants, and attractions in many cities.

- Free maps. While we're all reliant on GPS, it never hurts to have a paper map in the car to help you find your way. CAA and AAA members can request free maps and guidebooks from their local branch.

- Military discounts. If you are serving a member of the military or a veteran who has retired from active service, many businesses offer you discounts.

- Union discounts. If you are a member of a union, consult your union's website for information on available discounts. Often, hotels, restaurants, and other businesses will offer a reduced rate. Some deals will be available year round and others are seasonal — often related to union meetings in the area.

- Senior discounts. While the age of retirement might be 65, people as young as 55 are often offered senior discounts. Some places will even offer a deeper discount for those over 85. (I like to call these folks super seniors.)

- Airport parking coupons. Look online before you head to the airport and you'll find many airport parking lots offer discounts if you print the coupon a day or more before your travel days.

- Hotel conference rates. If you're traveling to attend a convention or conference, the event organizers have likely organized a block of rooms held at a reduced rate. Take advantage of the savings.

- Online deals. While you'll need to use your internet savvy about online travel deals, check for better rates either with the hotel directly or through services such as Expedia, Hotwire, and Trivago.

- Ask the concierge. Front desk staff at your hotel may be able to offer you discount coupons or free passes for local restaurants and tourist attractions.

International travel:

- Find your passport. Nothing derails a cross-border trip faster than missing identification documents so keep yours in a safe place to help you find it when you're ready to go.

- Passport expiry dates. You likely know that you can't travel on an expired passport. However, be alert that many countries deny you permission to visit if your passport is within six months of expiry. Start the renewal process 9 to 12 months before your current passport expires to ensure you always have current travel documents.

- Use NEXUS. If you live in Canada or the United states, you can apply for a Nexus card to use faster lineups at land and air border crossings. Time savings for the win!

- Check for travel advisories. Health restrictions, natural disasters, warfare, and more can make it unsafe to travel to certain destinations. Check current advisories from the Government of Canada (travel.gc.ca/traveling/advisories), the U.S. Department of State (travel.state.gov/content/travel/en/traveladvisories/traveladvisories.html/) and other officials before your trip.

Moving forward, keep hotels in mind, if you need some extra workspace. Dr. Maya Angelou famously "kept a hotel room in every town [she] ever lived in," noted Julie Zevelof for *Business Insider* ("Maya Angelou Always Rented A Hotel Room Just For Writing," BusinessInsider.com, May 28, 2014), as a home away from home writing studio – even when she had a home in the same city.

As the travel industry explores new business models, more hotels may follow Zoku Amsterdam's example with rooms "designed specifically for remote workers and digital nomads. It fits space-saving 'loft' apartments into the plots of standard hotel rooms, has a coworking space instead of a lobby" writes Lauren Razavi for DigiDay ("Remote work has kickstarted a hotel subscription-living movement," March 1, 2021). Having a room on retainer could be a useful option to keep working if your home office loses power or internet access. It can also create a comfortable place to retreat during extreme weather events.

11
What (Not) to Wear

Working from home gives us more options about what to wear to work. Shoes are now optional if you want to wear your cozy slippers all day. That reflects a trend towards more casual dressing while in your home office. Some would say too casual, if pajamas and grubby t-shirts are the new normal. Then again, maybe you have daytime pajamas that are suitable for your style at work.

The Wall Street Journal reported on research that suggests "your clothing choices at home affect productivity and performance" a phenomenon known as "enclothed cognition." ("The Science Behind WFH Dressing for Zoom," *The Wall Street Journal*, September 20, 2020). It's an interesting notion to consider the power of your wardrobe choices and how that can affect you. While a nice blouse and some makeup might help you feel more professional, casual clothes signal to your mind and body that it's time to rest and relax. You may have to experiment to figure out what works for you.

That said, what you wear is nobody's business. You've got a body in your unique size, shape, and weight and you get to dress in ways that make you feel good. Bra or no bra? Soft cotton sweaters or scratchy wool blazers? Clean shaven or scruffy beard? The choice is yours, for the most part. What you wear and your personal hygiene should aspire to, at least, a minimally acceptable professional appearance. You can still wear your slippers and look great on video chat!

1. Dress for Your Job

Figuring out what to wear to work can be an exercise in frustration. When you commuted to work, you had to pick one outfit for the entire day including shoes and coat. Often, it was hard to balance what you needed throughout the day. You might have carried a heavy rain coat for torrential rain as well as an extra pair of shoes so you didn't have to squelch around the office in wet shoes. In summer, a light shirt and pants might have been sufficient on the commuter train but you had to bring a sweater and scarf to combat the office air conditioning. There's a reason why some commuter trains often smell of body odor!

Now that you work from home, you still have to get dressed but, in theory, the frustrations are less. At first, it feels like freedom to be able to wear whatever you want. However, that might not be professional nor productive. Vanessa Bohns, associate professor of organizational behavior at Cornell University, "recommends changing into clothing associated with work at the beginning of the day to cue a sense of being in serious work mode." ("The Science Behind WFH Dressing for Zoom," *The Wall Street Journal*, September 20, 2020). So, even if you work from home, getting dressed for work helps ensure you're ready to work during office hours. However, you need to dress for your job. Even remote workers will want to fit into the corporate or brand style. Compare an IT company's staff who favor golf shirts to a makeup company's employees who embrace the latest fashions. There's a huge scope of possibilities from casual to professional.

Casual dress is a matter of perception. Do you consider a polo shirt and jeans casual? How about yoga pants and a tank top? Or pajamas and a housecoat? Are pants optional? See what I mean? There are different degrees of casualness. Within the conventions of your corporate culture, you will decide how to dress down (and dress comfy!) as much as you feel comfortable in front of your colleagues.

On the other end of the spectrum is professional dress. Lawyers and their clients appearing before a judge will wear tailored suits or something similar, even if the hearing is held over video chat. Doctors doing telehealth medicine might wear scrubs or a white lab coat; both are equally professional attire for the medical industry. Yet again, some companies expect their employees to wear uniforms — matching T-shirts, maybe — even if all their customer contact is over video chat.

Now, professional clothes don't have to be dressy or a specific uniform. Take a peek at my author photo and you'll see my professional style; something I call "professor casual." (For the record, I am a postsecondary instructor but I am not a professor, a credentialed honorific designation at Canadian universities.)

Overall, you have to decide what is appropriate dress for your job.

2. Consider Video Chat

Before you fully commit to your outfit for the day, glance at your calendar to see if you have any video meetings scheduled. If you do, you might want to give your outfit a second look to make sure it will work on camera.

On a recent Facebook Live, Trinny Woodall, founder and CEO of Trinny London, a UK-based cosmetics company, noted "[On a Zoom call], you want to be noticed enough in what you're wearing that people might call you out for your opinion" (Facebook Live, February 20, 2021). Later in the same broadcast, she added "When all else fails, put on your best color; the color that you can wear without any makeup ... where you look good."

Excellent tips for starters!

I've put a lot of time into Zoom calls and video teaching, so I will add more tips:

- Try to avoid stripes and busy patterns. They often appear to move on camera which is distracting for your viewers.

- Remember that strapless tops will make you look naked if just your head and shoulders are on video.

- Use moisturizer or makeup, if you like, to give your face some color and glow. Without it you may look tired, even if you're not sleepy.

- If you use makeup, focus on lips with a bright shade so that people can more easily lip read what you're saying if the audio is scratchy.

- If you want to make a fashion statement, focus on things the viewer will see such as earrings, hair accessories, a necklace, a scarf, or a branded company shirt, depending on your situation.

- Reflect on the consequences if you only dress your top half. Is there a risk your co-workers will see your saggy jogging pants or, perhaps more embarrassing, your underwear?

- If your home office is chilly, keep a lap blanket nearby so that you don't have to shroud the visible part of yourself in a giant scarf.

At the end of your work day, take time to change out of your work clothes whether they are casual, professional, or something in between. "What you wear can also make a difference when it's time to wind down. Putting on your relaxation clothes or your at home clothes, shifts your brain into 'I can relax now. I can shift gears. I don't have to be operating at this high cognitive level,'" says organizational psychologist Cathleen Swody. "It's like the Mister Rogers effect." ("The Science Behind WFH Dressing for Zoom," *The Wall Street Journal*, September 20, 2020.)

Section 3
Soft Skills

Now that you've worked your way through the practical decisions necessary to work from home, it's time to consider some of the soft skills that make us more efficient, more productive, and, often, happier in our work.

One of the biggest challenges you'll face is how to hold boundaries around your working life. You want to integrate work and life without running the risk that life will prevent you from doing your work. It's a tricky problem.

In addition, you'll develop strategies to be more productive so that you can manage your time and stay on track with your most important tasks. Productivity is about finding the methods that will best suit you. There are lots of different approaches you could use.

Your soft skills will also include interpersonal relationships. How you communicate with colleagues and clients is even more important when you're not in the same office with them. Additionally, it's important to think about diversity, equity, and inclusion. Just as you want to be included, you'll need skills to ensure everyone has equitable access to the work you do.

Finally, we'll wrap up the book with a look at strategies to support your health. When home and work are integrated, it's important to prioritize healthy habits that support your mental, physical, and spiritual wellness. We need you fit so you can do your work and enjoy your life.

There's a lot left to cover, so let's get to it.

12
Boundaries

No matter where you work, boundaries are those intangible things that define how, when, and where you work. At a conventional office, it's understood everyone's in work mode until the end of the day. Working at home doesn't offer up those same signals unless you put them in place.

Once you decide what boundaries you will need when working from home, setting these boundaries is the easy part — holding them is easier said than done and it takes practice and persistence to get them right.

1. Office Hours

Time is a great boundary. You can use the calendar and the clock to determine when you're at work even though you're at home. It's up to you to decide if you work Monday to Friday or Wednesday to Saturday. You can start at 5:00 a.m. or noon or 6:00 p.m. as suits you and you get to determine how long (or short) your office hours are.

In an ideal world, work time is uninterruptible but we don't live in an ideal world. The phone will ring, the doorbell will chime, your child will need help, your roommate will turn the TV on full volume, or any of a thousand other interruptions. Even our technology is designed to continually distract us with the buzzes and beeps associated with incoming email, text messages, and social media posts. Even if you've silenced your mobile phone and muted your computer, you can still be interrupted by visual notifications — flags and pop ups that light up your screen. Your goal is to manage those interruptions during work time so you can focus on work.

Using time as a boundary can also help you transition from work mode to home mode and you can use it as a tool to let your family or roommates know when you're "at home" for domestic issues and social time.

Many people who work at home choose to work all day every day. That's great if it's your choice and you want to be at your desk anytime, any day. However, I also want to remind you that you are allowed to set and hold hours of work. As Twitter user @LoveStats tweeted, "Just because everyone else seems to be stunningly passionate about their job 24/7 doesn't you do too. You can like most of your job most of the time, forget about it during your personal time, and still feel good about yourself."

2. Real or Virtual Commute

How's your commute? My last conventional office job had me commuting from my suburban home into downtown Vancouver three days a week. Due to my childcare arrangements, I couldn't catch the high-speed commuter train's last departure each morning and the only available bus route took two hours and thirty minutes each way so I had to drive. I traveled along an urban stretch of the Trans-Canada Highway during peak hours. A typical commute was 90 minutes getting to the office and roughly 60 minutes coming home again. When I decided to work from home I recouped 7.5 hours per week — the equivalent of 31 percent of my working hours at the time. In retrospect, the amount of time I spent commuting was insane, not to mention terrible for the environment!

Giving up the commute is a big catalyst for many people who decide to work from home. However, there's a risk that you'll spend the time saved on commuting working extra unpaid hours. Reflect on whether you want to extend your business day or whether you want to use those hours for leisure pursuits.

Whether you drive to work, bike to work, or take public transit, that time between work and home creates a useful buffer. Working from home eliminates the commute time and comes with substantial cost savings if you no longer need a commuter vehicle or monthly transit pass. However, we need to remember the benefits of our commute time, not just the drawbacks. Consider these benefits of commuting:

- A chance to rest your mind and do nothing.

- An opportunity to daydream or brainstorm.

- Time to socialize with friends on the same commute.

- A chance to shake off the stresses of home or office.

- Listening time for music or podcasts to inform, entertain, or enlighten.

- Time to get some steps in walking to the bus stop or up from the parkade.

- An opportunity to be anonymous and untethered.

If we eliminate the traditional commute as we work from home, a virtual commute helps us retain the benefits of commuting. Casually known as a fake commute or a faux commute, here are some ways to retain the benefits of commuting and create boundaries around your work hours at home:

- Go for a walk around your neighborhood.

- Create a distraction-free reading nook and spend 30 minutes reading.

- Start your day with a pre-work latte from your favorite coffee shop.

- Listen to one podcast episode before and after work.

- Put on your favorite tunes and dance to three songs.

- Walk around your backyard or patio garden and water the plants.

- Set up (and, at the end of the day, tear down) your videoconference equipment.

- Drive somewhere for "office treats" every Friday. (I love a good donut!)

3. Domestic Distractions

When you work at home, your home can become a distraction! You might feel compelled to empty the dishwasher or run a load of laundry instead of sitting down to your work. Essential tasks such as making a grocery list, checking the smoke detector, and sorting your recycling can feel more important than your work. You might even feel compelled to complete nonessential tasks like color-sorting your books, trimming your hedge, or deep cleaning your garage. I know I'm in trouble when I feel compelled to rearrange my office library!

One of the joys of working from home is that we can tuck domestic tasks in the gaps for our work. Sort your laundry before breakfast and it's not hard to fling a load in the washer, then dryer, during the work day. The difficulty comes when the domestic chores breach your work boundaries and your work doesn't get done.

These domestic distractions fall neatly under the notion of resistance, a term coined by Steven Pressfield in his book *The War of Art*. Pressfield writes, "Resistance cannot be seen, touched, heard, or smelled. But it can be felt. We experience it as an energy field radiating from a work-in-potential. It's a repelling force. It's negative. Its aim is to shove us away, distract us, prevent us from doing our work." (*The War of Art*, Black Irish Entertainment LLC, 2002.) By acknowledging the things that create resistance around us, you are better equipped to ignore them, overcome them, and get back to work.

4. People Distractions

The people around you will likely be the biggest source of distractions. They will also be the most tenacious as they try to breach your work boundaries over and over again. Children wanting a snack, spouses who want to talk about retirement planning, roommates who want to complain that someone (you?) ate their leftovers; every person in your household will override the boundary at some point.

Friends and neighbors may also struggle to understand that when you work at home you're really working. You'll be hit up for favors to fetch courier packages, feed pets, and bring in the garbage bins. Imagine leaving the office to pick up someone else's relative at the airport! While it's good to be neighborly, too much help during work hours risks your ability to get things done.

4.1 Children

Parenting while working from home is an extra special challenge made all the more difficult as children change over time and your boundaries will have to evolve, too. Your kids need you whether they're big kids or little kids. It's just what they'll need that will shift as they get older.

Some child-related distractions are predictable and we can plan to minimize them. "If you've got older children, understanding the nature of interruptions can help you minimize them. Take notes for a few days. If you're frequently asked for snacks, maybe they need to be made more accessible. If you're doing tech support, try teaching a troubleshooting session. Check the inventory of school supplies. Post the day's meal menu in the kitchen. You might also decide that certain bids for attention are best met. Online learning gets lonely (just as working from home gets lonely), recommends Laura Vanderkorn." ("6 strategies for parents struggling with work-from-home interruptions," *The Washington Post*, January 25, 2021.)

Even if you work from home, you may still want to invest in childcare. Depending on where you are and assuming lack of childcare options isn't the reason you work from home, see if you can arrange something like these options:

- Trade babysitting with a neighbor.

- Book before and after schoolcare.

- Find a placement in a daycare facility.

- Hire a babysitter.

- Put a nanny on payroll.

If both parents work from home or another work-from-home parent lives near you, Laura Vanderkam suggests a scheduled childcare swap. She writes, "Consider an 8:00 a.m. to 6:00 p.m. workday. This can be split into two shifts: 8:00 a.m. to 3:00 p.m., and 1:00 p.m. to 6:00 p.m., with each parent alternating who gets which shift (1:00 p.m. to 3:00 p.m. is nap time for little kids, or screen time for older kids, so it can be double-booked, with the 8:00-3:00 parent providing 'if need be' supervision). When each party truly covers — keeping the kids out of the other party's hair — each parent will get 25 fully focused, predictable work hours each week, and four to six probable hours with the nap swaps." ("6 strategies for parents struggling with work-from-home interruptions," *The Washington Post*, January 25, 2021.)

For those situations where childcare doesn't fit your budget or occasional days when childcare falls through, here are some things you could try:

- Take a day off work to focus on parenting.

- Have a "take your child to work" day.

- Give them toys to mimic your work — to small children, work is play! Toy giant Fisher Price even has a "My Home Office" set for sale. Older kids love to use office supplies.

- Have older children look after younger siblings.

- Work in bursts of time while children are busy with an activity.

- Communicate time and let children know when you'll next be available.

- Use a sign on your office door to communicate your status; a stop sign or a clock can show readers and non-readers your status.

You'll find some ready to print signs on the downloadable forms kit accessible through the link at the back of this book, such as a stop sign, a Do Not Disturb door hanger, and a digital clock. Print them out and use them as is. If possible have the printouts laminated so that they last longer and you can write on them with a dry-erase marker.

Work-from-home dad Sergei Urban offered a refreshing perspective when it comes to kids and video calls. On his Facebook page, TheDadLab, he wrote, "Do you know the feeling when your child comes into the room while you are in the middle of an important zoom call? I had that experience the other day, and my instinct reaction was to find a way to hide him from the video because I got used to the idea that I should not mix my professional life with a personal one. But then, I started thinking that all people on that call are probably in exactly the same position being at home and balancing family responsibilities with work … so why is it a problem when my kids appear in my video calls from time to time? At that moment, I decided to embrace this new reality. I have introduced my son to the meeting. He waved 'hello,' and then he was off to continue his own adventures. As for me, I don't feel guilty about this situation happening anymore. We can change the norm."

One last thought: Maybe we need to rethink how parents work and the way professional expectations intgrate with family life. In an opinion piece for CBC News, journalist Amy Bell posed the question "Is working from home actually working for anyone?" (CBC News, May 23, 2020). She explored the challenges working at home presents for parents, especially women, and concluded that "The government, employers and employees need to realize that the real work we need to do is dismantling the expectations we have of ourselves when it comes to both work and parenting. And to work on solutions that — going forward — will not only be sustainable but beneficial to both sides."

4.2 Adults

Adults can be just as distracting as kids. Whether you live with your spouse, adult children, elders, or roommates, they all have the potential to breach your work boundaries. Often they interrupt with things that could wait until later and may not realize the negative impact on your work.

You can't manage adults the same way you do children but here are some things you can do :

- Focus on what's most important: safety, sleep, hydration, food, comfort. Remember that Maslow's hierarchy of needs does not include Wi-Fi.

- Be kind: If emotions are running high, sometimes it's best to accept the interruption to reduce stress and worry.

- Pause before you react: Count to five or take deep breaths before you turn away from your computer and react to the interruption. Remember you live with these people!

- Practice patience: It may take a while before adults in your life understand that you're working and shouldn't be disturbed. Acknowledge the learning curve.

- Pick your battles: If an elderly relative interrupts you daily at 11:00 a.m. with a cup of tea, go with the flow and take a short break from work.

- Communication is key: Talk about what you need to get your work done. Keep talking to solve problems. Be clear: "I need to focus on work today. I will be done at 4:00 p.m. and we can discuss anything you need to then."

- Vent when you need to, but be mindful of your audience: Try to do it in private so there are no hard feelings.

- Avoid unnecessary arguments: This might mean letting go of some household decisions.

- Acknowledge differences: Different adults have different abilities. Not all people are neurotypical. You may need to adapt your work boundaries while they're around.

- Keep money in mind: Protect your work time. If you compromise too often, you'll jeopardize your income.

5. Neighborhood Distractions

Your home office may be set up well for your work but your neighborhood might add a few glitches to your productivity. You'd expect to navigate normal levels of traffic noise, children playing, dogs barking occasionally, and more. The problem is when the distractions get bigger and when their frequency increases.

I've experienced many distractions in my suburban home office and I do my best to work around them. I know on Tuesday mornings, the garage and recycling trucks are in my neighborhood. I start work later in the day on Tuesdays. I know it takes my neighbors about 30 minutes to mow their lawns. When they mow, I take a long coffee break. If your neighbors have bigger lawns that take longer to mow, invest in some noise-canceling headphones. Revisit Chapter 4 for more on technology that can help you. Keep in mind some distractions are more urgent; I once had to rush outside and ask my neighbor to pause his power washing so I could do a live radio interview. You'll adapt as best you can, too.

Many neighbors might not realize you work from home. While it's an increasingly common work arrangement, not everyone is familiar with it. Communicate with your neighbors and work together to come up with plans that work for everyone. Most people are pretty accommodating.

One last thought: Women often put other people's needs before their own. If that sounds like you, spend some extra time defining your boundaries and make a plan to stick to them.

6. Negotiate Your Boundaries

As you've just read, holding boundaries has a lot to do with negotiation. Take time to understand others' needs and to communicate your needs. With a mutual understanding, you can work out solutions to suit your circumstances.

6.1 Negotiation strategies

While you may be an experienced business negotiator, take care not to apply the same aggressive negotiating tactics you might use to close a business deal. Negotiating with your cohabitants requires a gentler approach. Here's a business school refresher: There are three approaches to negotiation — soft, hard, and principled.

Hard negotiations are best reserved for situations from which you are willing to walk away. For example, a company manufacturing computer parts will pit one supplier against another to get the best possible price. When negotiating work-from-home boundaries, you can't threaten to walk away from the deal.

Soft negotiations involve give and take. One party yields to the needs of the other on some things. In doing so, they forego their original position and accept that they'll get slightly less than they wanted. For example, you might want to serve seafood at your next catered client event but the caterer can only supply chicken to stay on budget. You concede to having chicken (giving up your desire for seafood) in order to keep your other desire — to stay within your budget.

The third type is principled negotiation. This is considered best practice as it looks to make a deal that suits everyone without anyone feeling hurt, angry, or taken advantage of. This type of negotiation focuses on objective interests. For example, if you and your spouse both work from home, you will work together to negotiate a work schedule and concurrent child care that ensures your children are safe and happy while you both achieve your work goals.

6.2 Negotiation tactics

As you talk with your roommates, family, or neighbors to agree on boundaries, there are many different negotiating tactics you could try. These include:

- **Compromise.** You want to work in the dining room while your roommate wants to set up a board game on the dining room table. You agree to stop work at 3:00 p.m. on Friday so your roommate can set up the game for the weekend. In turn, the roommate agrees that the table will be available for work again by 8:00 a.m. Monday morning.

- **Yield.** Sometimes you have to give up something that's less important to you in order to get what you want. You may want to work at your desk in silence but your spouse needs to work at their desk on a series of conference calls. You temporarily yield either your desk or your desire for silence.

- **Problem solve.** All parties work together to find solutions so that you don't have to negotiate. For example, if your work and your child's virtual lessons conflict, consider relocating your office to another part of the house or move the lessons from dining room to rec room.

- **Do nothing.** If you're not sure how to approach a negotiation or you need more time to prepare, inaction delays the discussion until you're ready to negotiate. For example, imagine you want your teen to spend less time gaming after school so you can use your internet access capacity to work. Rather than use your parenting capital on this issue, you do nothing, for now.

6.3 Best Alternative to a Negotiated Agreement (BATNA)

Sometimes negotiation doesn't happen at all or the results don't go your way. That can be frustrating, especially when your work is so closely tied to the rest of your life. To help prevent that frustration, use the best alternative to a negotiated agreement (BATNA) strategy. BATNA was first introduced by negotiation researchers Roger Fisher and William Ury in their bestselling book, *Getting to Yes* (Penguin Books, 1981). Think of BATNA as an insurance policy if negotiation is a struggle.

BATNA means you reflect on the possible outcomes prior to the negotiation and decide in advance what result you can live with and what the consequences might be. Often reflecting on the BATNA will make you realize that you don't need to proceed with the negotiation. It can also help you develop a deeper understanding of your position and assist you in deciding what negotiating tactics will be most effective to find a resolution.

6.4 Documentation strategies

Whatever the outcome of your negotiations, take time to document the results so everyone shares a mutual understanding of decisions made. Here are some examples:

- Document childcare schedules, meeting schedules, or other date/time specific information on a calendar. It's easier to update and share digital calendars but paper calendars can be equally effective.

- Write up a short memo to capture the points you've discussed. Add signatures to the document to turn it into a contract. As it's not a legally binding agreement, even children can sign it, assuming they were part of the negotiations.

- Record a video or audio file of a conversation summarizing the agreement. The file is date and time stamped and can be replayed as evidence, if need be.

Taking time to document the boundaries you've agreed on will give you something concrete to reference. This will help you hold those boundaries in place and show you where further negotiation is needed.

13
Productivity

Contrary to lots of online advice, there is no one-size-fits-all productivity solution. To be productive, you're going to have to figure out what works for you, your workspace, the kind of work you do, and the people around you.

Sometimes productivity is variable. You'll have good days and not-so-good days, busy weeks, and vacation weeks, and that's okay. Nobody is productive all the time. In fact, part of productivity is making sure you have some downtime for rest and recreation, too.

Anita Adams, an independent consultant with Rodan+Fields, wrote "I've worked from home now for 20 years and I absolutely love it."

Sometimes it can be challenging though – like finding the motivation to get the stuff done that you don't really want to do particularly when the sun is out and you just want to go play.

"Here's my secret that helps me get through those days. Pull out your calendar and make sure you block out a chunk of time for you to do something fun at least a few times a week (or daily if you can). When I know I can slip out for a walk or a kayak in the afternoon, it helps me get laser focused on what needs to get done."

"It also really helps to know when you are your most productive. For me, that's in the morning so I typically do my business building activities before noon and then leave the afternoon open for some play time and filling in the gaps."

1. Work on Your Workflow

To be productive, you've got to find your workflow. Seek the combination of routines, habits, schedules, and tools that let you get the right things done. If you're an early riser, maybe you work from oh-dark-early until breakfast. If you're a night owl, like me, you might work later in the day to get the most done. If you've got kids, your schedules probably aligned with their activities.

One of the longstanding myths about working from home is the notion that workers are less productive away from a traditional office. It's simply not the case. Rather, people who work at home have a variety of different workflows. Many of them are unfamiliar until you've experienced them. Let's break this myth once and for all: Work at home workers are productive!

Your workflow isn't just about how you use your time, it's also about having the tools and information to do your work. Should you have client files or other resources at hand? Are you a maker who needs fabric, paint, or other materials nearby? Whatever you do or make, set yourself up for success by having the materials organized in or near your workspace. If space is an issue, set out what you need for the day first thing so you can work without having to resupply.

If your work is digital, make sure you have a system in place to access your work on all the devices you'll be using to get the job done. If files move between you and your colleagues, figure out access that works for everyone such as cloud storage or a central server accessed over VPN. Stay mindful of version control so that no work is wasted sorting out conflicting, partially updated, partially outdated documents.

Tools such as Trello can be used to create virtual job boards for your projects. Even a simple Kanban-inspired system using lists for To Do, Doing, and Done items can keep work flowing. Alternatively, you might need a communication solution such as Slack if your email inbox is bursting at the seams.

2. Be Alert to Distractions

When you work at home, it takes practice and discipline to ignore distractions and remain productive. Household chores such as cleaning the bathroom, loading the dishwasher, and keeping up with the laundry can all erode your work time. Other people in your home can also be a distraction whether you live with your chatty mother-in-law or have three kids to care for while you work. Your personal interests may also distract you — the latest episode of your favorite TV shows on the PVR, personal social media feeds, or your fitness room might tempt you to play instead of work during office hours.

Be cautious of household or personal tasks that don't have to be done during work time. If you need to clear the mental clutter to get on with your work, designate a whiteboard, Post-it Note pad, or digital to-do list, to take note of the task then plan to deal with it on a break or after work.

Set boundaries and stick to them (refer back to Chapter 12).

Careful not to distract yourself: You can get derailed looking for an email attachment to complete your current tasks, if you detour to triage your inbox or archive old messages.

3. Have Systems

Efficient work is about finding the systems that work for you. Some people live for to-do lists while others work best from a schedule. When you work at home, you get to choose the work patterns that fit your life. The key is to find a flexible system that will allow you to integrate work and life.

Productivity expert, Mike Vardy's TimeCrafting system is a great example. Here's how Mike describes it: "TimeCrafting is a philosophy and framework developed over the past decade in my work as a productivity strategist. At its core, TimeCrafting creates waypoints to guide your time and your tasks using several interconnected elements — themes, modes, and reflection.

"Themes, such as family day or video month, create a focal point for you to make progress on your projects and goals. Modes help you filter tasks according to available energy resources treating yourself and your to-do list better in the process. For example, if you're tired after a long meeting, you could focus on low energy mode tasks while you recover. With TimeCrafting, you then combine these elements with deeper reflection, something that will allow you to stay the course you've plotted for yourself and your work (or course correct if you've veered off target).

"TimeCrafting is a simple, flexible, durable, and sustainable system. Using this system, people all over the world spend less time "doing" productive and more time "being" productive — no matter what their work is and where they do it."

I'm a big fan of Mike Vardy's work and — full-disclosure — a member of TimeCrafting Trust, a community of professionals from many different industries who all use the TimeCrafting system. Learn more at productivityist.com.

3.1 Time

Think about how time works in your job. Are you tackling a list of tasks that can be done anytime? Or are you locked into a rigid client schedule where you have to greet Mrs. Parikh at 11:00 a.m.? Perhaps, you're somewhere in between with some scheduled meetings and some flexibility to get tasks done.

3.2 Tasks

Another necessary system is some sort of task tracking. Essentially, this tracking is your professional to-do list so that you know what work needs to be done. Some tasks repeat daily: check email, return phone calls, review social media, and so on. Other tasks are unique to whatever project you're working on. Typically, projects are too big to complete in a single day so you'll need to know how to break the task down into more manageable subtasks. In the tools section to follow, you'll find suggested ways to keep track of your tasks.

3.3 Tools

Whether you're tracking time or tracking tasks, you'll need tools to help you remember what to do when. While we live in the digital age, many people, including me, use analog solutions such as paper planners and whiteboards. I find I'm most productive when I keep a digital calendar and a paper task list. Likely, you'll use a combination of digital and analog tools in your work.

In terms of time, scheduling apps such as Google Calendar or Outlook calendar can help you manage your appointments and recurring events with ease. You may also want a desk calendar or pocket calendar to make notes or simply to have that satisfying feeling of crossing something off your list.

You can also use time-management apps throughout the day. Tomato Timer, for example, will guide you through Pomodoro-style work sprints. There's also Timeular, an app that helps you track time with the flip of an eight-sided tracking dice.

For task management, again, there are digital solutions such as Asana, Trello, Google Keep, Workflowy, and more to keep you on track. You may have to experiment to see if you need the functionality of the more complicated tools.

4. Productivity Experts

Even if you know a lot about productivity and consider yourself a highly productive person, it's always a good idea to check-in with experts who study time and how we use it. Consult these experts from time to time to give your productivity a tune up:

- Mike Vardy (productivityist.com)
- Stephen Warley (lifeskillsthatmatter.com)
- Chris Bailey (alifeofproductivity.com)
- Courtney Carver (bemorewithless.com)
- Charlie Gilkey (www.productiveflourishing.com)

You'll find a list of additional productivity resources in the downloadable kit.

14
Diversity, Equity, and Inclusion

While your personal decision to work from home may or may not be driven by a need to accommodate your own mobility or energy, every worker has the opportunity to create a more inclusive workforce and, in turn, a more inclusive community. Acts of inclusion start with just one person: you. Everyone who works at home needs to be alert to the multiple facets of diversity, equity, and inclusion.

Even if you work alone at home, you'll have at least a few interactions with other people throughout the year. If you work with a team, you'll have more contact. That contact increases exponentially if you work with clients or customers on a daily basis. With all this interaction, you need to be aware of diversity, equity, and inclusion (DEI). In part, it's social signaling that you are aware of the issues and doing your part to meet today's social standards. However, it's also good business. Social-justice-savvy customers want to work with companies that embrace DEI. Who doesn't want more happy customers? More importantly, who doesn't want to live in a more inclusive society?

1. Who's Underrepresented, Misrepresented, or Missing?

Diverse members of the community are often underrepresented, misrepresented, or missing from workplace conversations. As a result, their contributions are overlooked or absent from business discussions, operational decisions, and much more. Work to improve these conditions is ongoing with the grassroots support from people like you who believe in social justice, a rapidly evolving movement affecting workplaces across North America and around the world.

You aren't required to attend community rallies or be a political activist to support diversity, equity, and inclusion. All you need is the belief that there is a wealth of experience, knowledge, and perspective available to improve the work you do and this can all be available to you and your business if you allow those who currently aren't involved to have a say. Your task is to increase your understanding and encourage relevant dialogue and action.

Ensure diverse voices, opinions, and perspectives are part of your business. To do that, you might speak up to create time for a nonverbal colleague to type their contribution in the chat. You could advocate for representation of a variety of skin tones, genders, and ages in your marketing materials. You could review your company's hiring policies to see if barriers exist that prevent qualified candidates from joining your team. Even a simple show of support by displaying a Pride flag, wearing an orange T-shirt, or some other symbolic action can help to foster inclusivity.

Doing this kind of advocacy work when you work from home can be challenging. You may need to advocate for yourself or, more commonly, you'll be in a position to advocate for others. It takes extra time and energy to speak up. Some workers feel afraid that they'll say or do the wrong thing so they do nothing instead. It's not easy.

Fortunately, you won't have to do a full research project to ensure your work helps foster a more inclusive society. For guidance, follow the work of leading DEI experts including Dr. Nika White (www.nikawhite.com) and Deborah Levine, editor-in-chief of American Diversity Report (americandiversityreport.com). For more resources, connect with organizations leading the way in DEI work:

- Canadian Centre for Diversity and Inclusion (ccdi.ca)

- National Diversity Council (www.nationaldiversitycouncil. org)

- Centre for Global Inclusion (centreforglobalinclusion.org)

- American Association of Access, Equity, and Diversity (www. aaaed.org)

You can't learn everything at once. After all, you have a job to do! However, please consider DEI as part of your ongoing professional development. You'll find a longer list of experts and resources in the downloadable kit.

2. Lenses for Diversity

Diversity is multifaceted. It comes in many different forms and there are myriad topics to consider. To navigate the social landscape, it's helpful to consider diversity through a series of lenses. Think of them like camera filters; additional layers of information about a person. I will discuss these filters in the next sections.

2.1 Cultural diversity

Cultural diversity embraces a person's ethnicity and heritage. Ask yourself what are this person's cultural norms and how are those norms expressed? Through this lens we observe the customs, dances, food, music, and other socio-cultural experiences. Language should also be considered as we look at language(s) spoken and their corresponding catch phrases, colloquialisms, and regional vernacular. Think about Indigenous, African, Chinese, Francophone, European, or other cultures. Further, consider if the person's life has included immigrant or refugee status, which would add another layer to their experience.

One way you can acknowledge cultural diversity is to acknowledge traditional territories at the start of any in-person meeting or virtual gathering. Territory acknowledgment is a centuries-old practice among Indigenous people. Taking time to do an acknowledgment honors the culture of your Indigenous colleagues and demonstrates respect to local First Nations. Consult the interactive tool at Native Land Digital, a nonprofit organization, to learn more about the land you work on: native-land.ca/resources/territory-acknowledgement.

2.2 Genetic diversity

Until fairly recently, genetic diversity was referred to as racial diversity. However, race is now considered an outmoded construct that wrongly categorized humans as Caucasoid (Caucasian), Mongoloid (Asian), or Negroid (Black). Research has confirmed that we are all genetic variations of the same human race. As such, the foundations of these categories have been debunked.

For this book, I've chosen to use the phrase "genetic diversity." However, the language is evolving in this area and will likely change in the years ahead.

Genetic diversity considers a person's physical traits as determined by their genes. Skin color, eye color, hair type, and more are a result of that genetic coding. Through heredity, different physical characteristics are associated with different groups of people. These include Indigenous, African, Asian, Latino, Caucasian, South Asian, and other labels. You may also hear the acronym BIPOC; this stands for Black, Indigenous, and Persons of Color.

2.3 Religious diversity

Religious diversity celebrates spiritual beliefs from organized religion to atheism. At work you may encounter Muslims, Sikhs, Buddhists, Christians, Agnostics, and Pagans as well as those who are spiritual without an affiliation to any organized religion. While you don't have to pry into their spiritual practices, it's more inclusive to acknowledge a wide range of high days and holy days across many religious practices. Friendly, respectful curiosity to learn more about religious festivals and beliefs can help, too.

2.4 Age diversity

From young to old, workplaces are filled with everyone from Gen Z to the Silent Generation. At work, it's important that we adapt to the different abilities and work styles of people in different age groups. Similarly, it's important to remember that workers are not inherently more or less skilled because of their age. Therefore, maturity or immaturity should not be used as an indicator of someone's abilities.

2.5 Ability diversity

Diverse physical and mental abilities are a staple of workplaces. Colleagues may be physically fit or living with a chronic condition that impacts their mobility, hearing, sight, or more. In parallel, colleagues' mental well-being may be impaired with a temporary bout of anxiety or an ongoing struggle with depression. Permanent cognitive impairments or neurodevelopmental conditions from birth, injury, or stroke may also need to be accommodated. The important thing is to focus on the adaptations needed — wheelchair, hearing aid, support animal, headphones and a quiet space — rather than defining the person by their different abilities.

2.6 Body type and personal expression

Whatever physical appearance your colleagues may have should be embraced. They might be tall or short, heavy or light, large or small, strong or weak, each with their own unique appearance. Varying forms of hair color, hair style, tattoos, piercings, clothing choices, and more are all part of their personal expression and sense of self. While every workplace has appearance conventions, remember to be compassionate and accepting of anyone who doesn't fit that cookie cutter mold.

2.7 Gender diversity and sexual orientation

Be alert to gender diversity and sexual orientation as another lens. Here, we consider lesbian, gay, bisexual, transgender, questioning, queer, intersex, pansexual, two-spirit (2S), androgynous, and asexual (LGBTQQIP2SAA+) communities.

2.8 Family diversity

With relationship statuses from single, married, divorced, widowed to "it's complicated," families come in myriad groupings. From nuclear families to multigenerational families to blended families to families by choice, your customers and your work colleagues could be living in dozens of different scenarios. Some families include children with one parent while others have two parents or more. Some include elders while others include family-by-choice who are more than just roommates.

2.9 Economic diversity

Finally, we look at economic diversity. Not everyone has the same financial obligations nor the same income. As a result, not everyone has the same opportunities such as postsecondary education or the opportunity to purchase a home. Try to avoid judgments based on clichés or stereotypes. For example, people who live in low-income areas being more likely to have a criminal record. It's just not true!

3. What to Do?

Once you have a sense of the different types of diversity, there's a lot to think about. While you shouldn't categorize and pre-judge your colleagues, and clients, these lenses give us a way to reflect on their perceptions and opinions based on the different experiences they've lived. Here are some ways you can put this awareness into action:

- Get to know colleagues socially, and actively listen to the personal stories they choose to share with you.

- Focus on the person, not the labels for their differences.

- Avoid making assumptions.

- Consult with local community members about best practices. Look to business associations, professional groups, and other public forums that offer ongoing professional development.

- Visit the library. Your local librarians are a font of knowledge!

- Browse local First Nations' websites. Do your research without burdening Indigenous people with your questions. Also, don't assume one Indigenous person will speak for a whole community.

- Arrange a meeting with a spiritual leader such as a priest, shaman, rabbi, or imam.

- Request feedback and act on it.

- Listen to what people intend to say. Sometimes they might have a hard time expressing their thoughts, so work with people to understand the true meaning behind their words.

- Be patient with yourself and others.

- Continue learning.

- Address your diversity policy with team members; encourage discourse from day one.

- Encourage your workplace to include diversity awareness and accessibility for all in your new staff onboarding.

- Have a diversity statement for your company (see section 3.1).

3.1 Diversity statements

Many companies are developing social justice statements and/or diversity statements to affirm their awareness of the diversity, equity, and inclusion and to communicate what actions they will undertake to address the related issues. These are typically public facing documents published alongside the mission, vision, and values statements we're all familiar with. The information is published on websites, social media, and other online channels and in annual reports, newsletters, and other print documents.

Individuals can also write diversity statements. This can be a useful exercise to clarify your understanding of the diversity lenses and to align your morals and values with your business self. Personal statements don't have to be published although some people share them on websites and social media.

Whether you're writing a diversity statement for yourself or your business, it's a living document that will evolve over time to state your values as they relate to diversity and frame those values in the context of work you do with diverse populations. Plan to review and update your document frequently to best reflect your current position and understanding. It's all in aid of a future of inclusivity.

Note: The thoughts in this chapter are offered in good faith and with good intentions. Please allow me to share my diversity statement (at time of writing) as a model. (To read the latest iteration visit angelacrocker.com/diversity-statement.)

> I believe Indigenous lives matter. I believe Black lives matter. I believe people of color matter. I believe women deserve equal pay for equal work. I believe love is love regardless of gender identity or sexual orientation. I

believe we should accommodate people with different abilities. I believe we should work from a place of curiosity and compassion. I commit to lifelong learning so I can know and do what's right each day moving forward. I believe we should lift one another up as often as possible and, in doing so, we all rise.

For more examples, visit blog.ongig.com/diversity-and-inclusion/ 10-examples-of-the-best-diversity-statements. Compiled by The Magnet, the blog of ONGIG job description software, you can read others' real diversity statements. I hope they inspire you to write your own.

15
Health and Wellness

Casually peruse your social media feeds and eventually a post will appear touting the value and importance of self-care. However, people who work at home soon realize that self-care isn't all bubble baths and meditation. Sometimes, self-care looks more like boring, practical things such as hiring someone to clean your home, ordering takeout for dinner a couple times a week, or bringing in experts to maintain your home (think gardener, plumber, etc.).

As you reflect on how to care for yourself, consider your well-being through three lenses — social-emotional wellness, mental health, and physical fitness. Read on for suggestions in all three areas.

1. Social-Emotional Wellness

When we work at home, we often work in isolation without the typical social connections and emotional support of office life.

You may miss the in-person camaraderie of celebrating a milestone achievement. You might also miss the opportunity to privately grumble about a rude customer. These social and emotional supports add to our sense of well-being. When we work alone or remotely, we have to take action to ensure we benefit from work relationships.

In general, social-emotional wellness is made up of several inter-connected components. In the context of working from home, we're going to look at five of them more closely.

First, consider **self-awareness** and assess your perception of your own emotions. Can you identify what you're feeling and why? Do you understand how your emotions affect your ability to do your work?

Next, reflect on **self-management**. Are you able to control your impulses? Can you take the initiative to get to work on a project and follow through on the commitment to get it done? Are you able to adapt your plans if circumstances change?

Then, think about **social awareness**. Can you perceive workmates' contributions to projects, even if you're physically apart? Are you able to look beyond yourself and see how others are coping? Can you appreciate the work other people are doing?

Extend your awareness to use your **relationship skills**. Can you build meaningful working relationships? (They don't have to be friendships.) Are you able to demonstrate empathy and compassion? Can you activate interpersonal communication skills to enhance those working relationships?

Finally, what types of **decision-making skills** contribute to your work? Are you good at problem-solving or do you have strong intuition? Can you demonstrate leadership? Apply creativity? Manage time effectively?

A balance of these social-emotional components gives you the capacity to function well at work (and at home). Here are some ways those feelings can manifest:

- You can talk about your emotions with colleagues.
- You can share your worries with others.
- You can relax in your off-hours.
- You are able to say no without guilt.
- You feel content most of the time.
- You feel supported in the work you do.
- You feel good about yourself.

2. Mental Health

Happily, mental health is increasingly a priority for entrepreneurs and employees.

In combination, mental health encompasses the cognitive, behavioral, and emotional elements of wellness. Work in general can create and exacerbate feelings of stress and anxiety. Working alone at home can add feelings of loneliness and isolation. Global affairs such as pandemics can also add layers of stress. It's important to address any mental health issues you may be experiencing.

The stress or anxiety can be triggered by many different things. You may have uncertainty about what you're tasked to do or be unsure about how much you are valued. You may also experience a loss of control or, perhaps, limited control about your work. Financial pressures, too, can compound the situation. Imagine if you go over budget or your start-up funding falls through. Even disruptions to your daily routine (remember boundaries?) and any health concerns you are experiencing can be triggers for stress and anxiety.

People who work at home are at risk of feeling loneliness and isolation. Without social contact at the office or any connection to other people during the work day, you may feel like you're on your own. Keep in mind that if you feel lonesome, others probably do too. One solution might be to reach out, if you can, to have a conversation or other connection with people.

While not an exhaustive list, here are a few mental health coping strategies that you could incorporate into your work routine when needed:

- Focus on what you can control.
- Adapt, if you can.
- Give your workday structure.
- Track your progress.
- Take breaks from email, social media, and other inputs.
- Include activities you enjoy in your daily life.
- Breathe. One breath at a time.

- Try square breathing. Inhale for 4 counts. Hold for 4 counts. Exhale for 4 counts. Hold for 4 counts. Repeat.

- Use this grounding technique: Look around and acknowledge five things you can see, four things you can touch, three things you can hear, two things you can smell, and one thing you can taste.

While stress, anxiety, loneliness, and isolation are among the most common mental health issues workers face, this is in no way an exhaustive list. Depression, eating disorders, panic disorders, obsessive-compulsive disorders, operational stress injuries, psychotic episodes, and more will all affect your ability to work.

You may have mental wellness concerns or be in a mental health crisis. Either way, it's vital that you get the support you need. Reach out to a friend, colleague, or family member for help. For clinical support, start with your family doctor or make an appointment with a counselor, psychologist, or psychiatrist. Seek a diagnosis if you don't already have one and you feel it's warranted, to better understand your mental health condition and take advantage of counseling, group therapy, medication, and any other support that may be available to you.

If you are experiencing any severe symptoms, dial 911 to request help from a first responder or go to your nearest emergency room. Here are some examples of severe situations where immediate help is needed:

- Thoughts of harming yourself or attempting suicide.

- Experiencing hallucinations or other sensations that can't be true.

- Making decisions that put you in danger.

- Inability to care for yourself.

- Suffering medication side effects.

- Drug or alcohol overdose.

- Imbibing dangerous combinations of drugs and/or alcohol.

It's also important to destigmatize mental health. Feeling anxious and needing medication to cope shouldn't be any different than suffering the flu and taking antiviral meds to help you recover. Don't let your fear of the diagnosis prevent you from seeking help.

Additionally, you may observe behavior in colleagues or employees that suggests they need support. Gently guide them to appropriate resources so they, too, get help when needed.

Some well-established, clinically sound apps are available to support your mental wellness. Try a free trial of Calm (www.calm.com) or Headspace (www.headspace.com) on iOS or Android. If you find it helpful, invest in a subscription. (I'm a big fan of Matthew McConaughey's sleep stories on Calm.) For a free option, explore Mindshift (www.anxietycanada.com/resources/mindshift-cbt) developed by Anxiety Canada, a nonprofit organization that advocates for mental health as priority and to erase any stigma or prejudice associated with mental health.

3. Physical Fitness

I like to joke that my job requires me to drive a desk. In a sense that's true, if I'm teaching a virtual lesson or working on my latest writing project, I am in my desk chair for hours at a time. However, long hours of sitting are not good for your body. Working on screens can trigger headaches. Leaning over your laptop can put strain on your neck. Inertia is bad for your heart health. Clearly, it's important to get up and move around. Our bodies are designed to be in motion.

Please note that I am not trained in kinesiology, nutrition, or medicine. The ideas presented in this chapter come from my own experience and observations. Any change to your physical fitness efforts should be made in consultation with a trainer or doctor who can formally access your unique needs. The key is to develop habits that keep you physically and mentally fit in whatever ways work best for you.

3.1 Movement

One of my favorite expressions is "movement is medicine." Stepping away from the desk for short breaks and taking on longer duration physical activities can counteract too much sitting. Try these easy options to get moving:

- Gently stretch your neck, arms, and legs.
- Do some yoga. Try a sun salutation for a full body stretch-and-strengthen.
- Rest your eyes. You can close them briefly or look off in the distance.
- Take a two-minute walk around your house.
- Go for a long walk around your neighborhood.
- Use your body for strength training. Try a quick set of squats, lunges, or planks between meetings.
- Do a video workout class — spin, aerobics, yoga, dance. I love the Broadway-inspired dance routines from 567 Broadway (www.567broadway.com).
- Join a sports team. Hockey, lacrosse, soccer, softball, and many other sports have community leagues.
- Sign up for skating lessons, pilates, aerobics, water running, or other indoor or outdoor group activities.
- Get up and dance to your favorite song.
- Try chair yoga at your desk.

A few simple movements throughout the work day can improve your physical comfort. If you're struggling to remember to get up from your desk, set an hourly alarm or invest in a fitness watch to remind you to move every hour. Don't forget to add some bigger workouts to your leisure time.

In partnership with Canada's National Arts Centre (NAC), MOOV Ottawa created a series of short dance videos to help viewers fit a fun five-minute movement break into their days. Dubbed Revive!, the videos explore stretching, house dance, and Waacking in brief five-minute "movement snacks." Suitable for all fitness levels, you can find them here: nac-cna.ca/en/video/series/revive.

3.2 Nutrition

Oddly, it can be easy to forget to refuel our bodies when we get sucked into the vortex of work onscreen. Fuel your body throughout the workday with nutritious nibbles. Here are some of my favorites for you to try:

- Fresh fruit or fruit salad

- Protein power smoothie

- Apple slices with peanut butter

- Crackers with cheese

- Sunflower seeds or pumpkin seeds

- Trail mix with dried fruit and nuts

- A small bar of chocolate

- Crudité with dip

You'll also feel better from day to day if you remember to hydrate. Drinking sufficient water can prevent headaches, aid digestion, fend off cramps, flush out toxins, and promote regularity. Feel free to drink other things, too. I often have a cup of tea on the go at my desk. However, be cautious about sugar and caffeine in drinks as too much can make you irritable, restless, or interfere with your sleep. That's why I usually drink decaffeinated tea!

3.3 Sounds and lights

From time to time, you'll consume digital content that includes audio or participate in yet another videoconference call. Be it a business tutorial or the latest episode of a motivational podcast, you'll turn up your speakers or plug in your headphones.

Be warned: Profound hearing loss can occur if you frequently listen at high volumes. When you work at home, there's no health and safety officer to check your decibel levels.

One key is to be alert to the volume. Extraneous noise nearby can have you turning up the volume. Let's say a healthy volume is four bars in a room with normal ambient noise. Try to stick with the same sound level if you're working on an airplane or in a loud coffee shop. If that's not loud enough, it's time to put on your noise-canceling headphones to improve sound clarity. If you don't, you'll be tempted to pump up the volume to hear your content. Do this cautiously and infrequently to protect your ears.

If you prefer to work in relative silence, noise-canceling headphones are a wonderful invention. Some noise-canceling headphones simply block the ear canal more fully. Others are powered by batteries and generate frequencies that cancel out common background noise frequencies. Neither will make your home office completely silent but it's a lot closer to quiet than no help at all.

Your eyes also need protecting when you work on screens most of the day. Eye-strain pain, headaches, and dry eyes are all common when we look at the screen too long. In part, this is because we tend to blink less than usual. The brightness of the screen and the lighting in the room can also cause glare that stresses our eyes.

Ideally, you'll give your eyes a rest at regular intervals to alleviate the problem. However, working at home means you're more likely to spend longer hours on screen. If you're experiencing long screen time hours each day, there are things you can do. For instance, many devices allow you to adjust the light emitted to exclude the blue end of the spectrum. Apple iOS and Android devices call this "night mode."

Alternatively, you may want to invest in glasses that include a blue light filter. Just as your sunglasses filter UVA/UVB rays, these filters reduce the amount of blue light that reaches your retina, the part of the eye most likely to be damaged.

Even more simply, you can train yourself to take mini breaks that adjust your range of vision. Gaze at photos of your children across the room or walk to the window and survey the horizon. Even closing your eyes for a few moments can change the focal length enough to give you a few minutes of recovery time. The Canadian Association of Optometrists notes, "Some optometrists recommend the use of the 20-20-20 rule. Every 20 minutes take a 20 second break and focus your eyes on something at least 20 feet away … This is intended to give your eyes a much-needed break." (opto.ca/health-library/computer-vision-syndrome-digital-eye-strain, accessed July, 2021.)

3.4 Sleep

Sleep. If you sleep, you'll be a better worker and a better person. When you're well-rested you communicate your ideas more clearly, get more done in less time, and make fewer mistakes.

Personally, I know it's time to stop writing when I start mixing up my homonyms. You'll have to trust me that I know the difference between there, their, and they're. Ditto for its and it's. But odds are if I've goofed, I was sleep deprived when I wrote it.

Do you know your tired-trigger errors? We've all done it. Pushed send on an email only then realizing we've quoted the wrong price. Uh oh! Or tweeted an autocorrect blunder? (I once left the "r" out of the phrase "little shirt"— oops!) Or tagged the wrong person? Or posted a personal post on a business page? Put the wrong address label on a shipment?

This is also a good time to think about how you handle criticism. When you're tired, it's not always easy to accept feedback with grace. A well-rested worker can handle criticism more easily. Fewer mistakes happen if you get a solid night's sleep.

Sleep is essential to a healthy life. It supports social-emotional wellness, mental health, and physical fitness. That necessity can easily be disrupted when we put too many hours into our work. Remember, starting early and ending late is not a sustainable business model.

As I mentioned earlier, blue light in the flow of computer monitors and mobile screens has detrimental effects. This includes a reduction in the production of melatonin, a hormone that regulates sleeping and waking patterns. Many people use screens in bed just before they try to fall asleep. (I see you reading just one more work email!) Tech-free time an hour or more before bed can improve your sleep. Some people accomplish this by keeping technology out of the bedroom entirely. Others have their devices in the room and use night mode, do not disturb, or airplane mode to limit the impact technology has on their sleep. Of course, in some cases, the phone must be on — especially for workers who are on call or those with family responsibilities.

You'll have to self-assess whether you have the discipline needed to resist the temptation to check a device that's nearby. You might want to extend that discipline to start your day without technology, too. Try early morning yoga, longhand writing, or cuddles with your pets or family instead.

If you find you can't get enough sleep overnight, I firmly believe that naps are good for you. If you work at home, you've got easy access to a cozy spot for siesta. A quick 20-minute snooze or a longer 90-minute power nap can refresh your mind and your body to continue through the rest of your day.

4. Look after Yourself

As you can see, health and wellness have many benefits for your mind and body. In turn, your health supports your ability to do your work. I love Alison Tedford's perspective on this. She enthused, "I consider myself to be my best business investment." Look after yourself to be more effective at work, even when work is at home.

You'll find links to more mental health resources in the downloadable kit.

Conclusion

Congratulations! You've done a deep dive into the wide range of options available to you as you work from home. Hopefully, you've made some decisions along the way and put this book down with a plan to enhance your work-at-home life. To help you keep track of what you've done and what's still on your task list, use the Work-from-Home Master Checklist. It'll set you up for success so that you can work in the zone as much as possible.

Know that it may take some time to find your work-at-home groove. It's not easy for every person nor every type of work. Remember, a virtual commute can be helpful to transition you from work mode to family mode and vice versa.

Be kind to yourself as you figure out what works for you. Be willing to adapt, as needed. As best you can, make a distinction between work time and home time.

Sample 4
Work-from-Home Master Checklist

If you decide to work from home, there are a lot of things to set up, track, and think about. Depending where you are in your plans, you may have some topics finished, others in progress, and still more on your to-do list. Track the progress on your work-from-home journey using this master checklist.

Introduction: Why Work from Home?

[ ] Employment Opportunities
[ ] Family Obligations
[ ] Medical Reasons
[ ] Financial Reasons
[ ] Job Perks

Chapter 1: What Does "Work from Home" Mean?

[ ] Remote Work
[ ] Entrepreneurial Work
[ ] Hybrid Work
[ ] Full Time or Part Time?

Chapter 2: Will the Work-at-Home Life Work for You?

[ ] Transportation
[ ] Productivity
[ ] Distractions
[ ] Boundaries and Transitions
[ ] Personal Needs
[ ] Meals and Refreshments
[ ] Health and Wellness
[ ] Fitness
[ ] Wardrobe
[ ] Savings and Expenses
[ ] Household Needs
[ ] Family Needs
[ ] Professional Opportunities
[ ] Communications
[ ] Social Connections
[ ] Technical Issues
[ ] Societal Perceptions

Chapter 3: Workspace

[ ] A Room of One's Own?
[ ] Environment Design
    [ ] Ergonomics
    [ ] Lighting (and Vision Care)
    [ ] Interior Design
    [ ] Sound
[ ] Accessibility
[ ] Hot Desks and Co-working Spaces
[ ] Meeting Space

Sample 4 – Continued

Chapter 4: Technology

[ ]   Consider Your Hardware
    [ ]   Computers
    [ ]   Mobile phones
    [ ]   Cameras
    [ ]   Peripherals
[ ]   Don't Forget the Software
    [ ]   Office applications
    [ ]   Data storage
    [ ]   Audio, video, and image editing
    [ ]   Website and content management
    [ ]   Antivirus, malware, and security software
    [ ]   Industry specific software
[ ]   Online Access

Chapter 5: Communication

[ ]   Virtual Meetings
[ ]   Live Video
    [ ]   Start with the basics
    [ ]   Find your gear
    [ ]   Consider distractions
    [ ]   Look after yourself
    [ ]   Final steps before you go live
[ ]   Messaging Etiquette

Ch 6 Hygiene, Privacy, Security, and Safety

[ ]   Health and Hygiene
[ ]   Privacy: Where Are You?
[ ]   Home Security
[ ]   Fire Safety

Ch. 7 Resources: Time, Talent, and Treasure

[ ]   The Time, Talent, and Treasure Trifecta
    [ ]   What about time?
    [ ]   Who has talent?
    [ ]   Treasure hunt
[ ]   Time, Talent, and Treasure Budgets
[ ]   What to Do When Resources Are Scarce

Ch. 8 Human Resources and Outside Experts

[ ]   Employees and Contractors
[ ]   Hiring Help
[ ]   Employee Files
[ ]   Nondisclosure Agreements
[ ]   Using Artificial Intelligence
[ ]   Human Resources (HR) Management Skills

Sample 4 – Continued

Ch. 9 Finance

[   ]   Budgets
   [   ]   Revenue
   [   ]   Expenses
[   ]   Bookkeeping
   [   ]   Statements
   [   ]   Payroll
[   ]   Loans and grants
   [   ]   Loans
   [   ]   Grants
[   ]   Taxes
[   ]   Insurance
[   ]   Business Banking and Expertise

Ch. 10 Business Travel

[   ]   How Often Will You Travel?
[   ]   Mobile Office
[   ]   Packing List
[   ]   Travel Tips

Ch. 11 What (Not) to Wear

[   ]   Dress for Your Job
[   ]   Consider Video Chat

Ch. 12 Boundaries

[   ]   Office Hours
[   ]   Real or Virtual Commute
[   ]   Domestic Distractions
[   ]   People Distractions
   [   ]   Children
   [   ]   Adults
[   ]   Neighborhood Distractions
[   ]   Negotiate Your Boundaries
   [   ]   Negotiation strategies
   [   ]   Negotiation tactics
   [   ]   Best Alternative to a Negotiated Agreement (BATNA)
   [   ]   Documentation strategies

Ch. 13 Productivity

[   ]   Work on Your Workflow
[   ]   Be Alert to Distractions
[   ]   Have Systems
   [   ]   Time
   [   ]   Tasks
   [   ]   Tools
[   ]   Productivity Experts

Sample 4 – Continued

Ch. 14 Diversity, Equity, and Inclusion

[   ]   Who's Underrepresented, Misrepresented, or Missing?
[   ]   Lenses for Diversity
     [   ]   Cultural diversity
     [   ]   Genetic diversity
     [   ]   Religious diversity
     [   ]   Age diversity
     [   ]   Ability diversity
     [   ]   Body type and personal expression
     [   ]   Gender diversity and sexual orientation
     [   ]   Family diversity
     [   ]   Economic diversity
[   ]   What to Do?
     [   ]   Diversity statements

Ch. 15 Health and Wellness

[   ]   Social-emotional Wellness
[   ]   Mental Health
[   ]   Physical Fitness
     [   ]   Movement
     [   ]   Nutrition
     [   ]   Sounds and lights
     [   ]   Sleep
[   ]   Look after Yourself

Download Kit

Please enter the URL you see in the box below into a web browser on your computer to access and use the download kit.

www.self-counsel.com/updates/workhome/21kit.html

The following are included on the download kit:

- Work from Home Self-Assessment
- Tech Shopping List
- Checklist for Tax Time
- More resources to help you as you work from home!